THE CASE AGAINST CHRIST

JOHN YOUNG

THE CASE AGAINST CHRIST

Some statements for the defence

HODDER AND STOUGHTON
LONDON SYDNEY AUCKLAND

British Library Cataloguing in Publication Data

Young, John, *1937 Feb 20–*
　The case against christ. – Rev. and enl.
　ed.
　1.Christianity
　I. Title
　200　　BR121.2

ISBN 0 340 39371 8

To Isabel, Debbie and Kate,
with thanks for your love and your laughter

FOREWORD
by Lord Blanch

I wish this book had been in my hands when I was a parish priest, because it answers questions my parishioners were asking – or would like to have asked. I wish it had been in my hands when I was a theological college principal, because the author handles important questions at a level those questions deserve. It would have been a good handbook for ordinands about to embark on their first curacy. For that matter I would have been glad to have had it when I was Archbishop of York; I could have saved myself a lot of long letters to irate critics of the Church and puzzled enquirers in search of faith. Altogether it is a remarkable achievement to have combined a lively, entertaining style with genuine scholarship, and a robust personal faith with openness to the objections and criticisms which may be urged against Christianity.

The author is chaplain and teacher in an academic establishment but, as he says, he does not live in an ivory tower. As one-time Chairman of the College I can vouch for his daily involvement in every aspect of college life, amongst the students and the staff. This book is the product of a lively intelligence, honest scholarship and personal commitment to Christ. The reader will learn a lot from this book about the Bible, about religion and science, about suffering and death, and about Christ and the resurrection – and he will learn, too, something about the author, a teacher, a thinker, a humble believer, a man mercifully endowed with a rare sense of humour. He has written the kind of book I would have expected him to write, and I whole-heartedly commend it to you. He has made out a good case for Christ.

Stuart Blanch
March 1986

WHAT THE REVIEWERS SAID ABOUT THE FIRST EDITION

"This is a fantastic little paperback."

Buzz

"A *must* for anyone who wants to get 'the gen' on popular objections to the Christian faith."

Crusader

"The writing is clear and concise, based on a considerable amount of scholarship, and the text is illustrated by some useful diagrams . . . a book to be recommended both to believers and non-believers."

Canon Paul Welsby, Chaplain to the Queen

"The uses of the book will be many – a general reference book . . . House groups . . . a Lent course."

The Reader

"Well worth getting and passing on."

Bishop Leslie Brown

"If there is a better book at answering popular objections to the Christian Faith, I'd like to see it."

Reconciliation Quarterly

"It really is superb."

Rev. Peter Bye

"A source of delight to me . . . I am going to make a second and third reading and so on."

A Doctor quoted by the Editor of *Challenge*

"The Devil has had a field day with the prejudiced assumption that you have to be some sort of moron to swallow Christianity. This little book does much to set the record straight and to demonstrate that, far from being in conflict, Christian faith goes hand in hand with reason, common sense, and historical fact."

Cliff Richard

"If ministers will put this book to use among all the members of their congregations, the result will be many less defensive Christians, better able to cope with the usual charges against their position."

Church of England Newspaper

* * *

The first edition of *The Case Against Christ* was published in 1971. It was reprinted three times (approaching a total of 50,000 copies). The book has been completely reworked and updated, and considerably enlarged, for this 1986 edition.

Contents

Thank You

Despite its modest size, a large number of people have assisted in the preparation of this book, and I gladly acknowledge their help.

For the typing of numerous drafts I am extremely grateful to Joyce Smith, and to Janet Vere and her marvellous team in the College Secretariat. For efficiency and sound advice, my thanks are due to Carolyn Armitage, the Editor. Stuart Blanch, Archbishop of York until 1983, kindly agreed to write a Foreword, and John Collins' fertile imagination has produced a series of lively drawings. I am indebted to them both – as I am to Rosie Congdon and Naomi Whitehead for checking the typescript, and to Patrick Duncan, Louise Redshaw and Harold Stutely for reading the proofs.

For perceptive comments and lively discussion of the various drafts I am tremendously grateful to Les Bingham, Peter Doble, David Gamble and Louise Redshaw. To protect their good names I should add that I didn't always take their advice. The book's limitations are mine, not theirs.

Above all I am indebted to Jackie Silins, my colleague in the Chaplaincy team, who helped in numerous ways, and to Stuart Coates, a post-graduate student at the College of Ripon and York St. John. Stuart has sifted, researched and double-checked a great deal of material. My confidence in the accuracy of the many facts contained within this book is due mainly to his initiative, industry and intelligence. In addition to their practical help, the supportive friendship offered by Jackie and Stuart – and many others – as I worked to meet deadlines was a considerable encouragement. My family has cheerfully endured my constant scribbling for several months, and to them I warmly dedicate the outcome.

John Young: York
January 1986

1

PLEASE START HERE

I often skip the first few pages of books – those sections with boring titles like Preface and Introduction. It is a foolish policy, because authors often give important clues to the way we should approach the book on our lap or at our bedside. So I hope you will read these first few pages – and the other pages too, of course!

About the author
The book will be more personal if I tell you a little about myself. And to further this aim I have asked John Collins to provide a portrait – very brave of me, for he is a cartoonist.

As you read, it will become obvious that I enjoy books. But I enjoy talking and listening even more, and many of the ideas in this book have come from numerous conversations.

I work in a college, and colleges are often defined as ivory towers – places where the pace of life is slow, and where all conversations are intensely intellectual. Such places may exist, but my college is not one of them!

My work brings me into daily contact with crowds of young people, and with large numbers of middle-aged and elderly people too – gardeners, caretakers, cleaners and highly qualified academics. Some students and colleagues share my faith; most don't.

Many conversations are about the weather, about the way the college is run, about football, about families. But quite often I discuss the Christian Faith with believer, agnostic and atheist. Whatever else I should like to claim for this book, I am sure of my ground when I claim this. The chapters which follow are based in the real world. The questions discussed are real questions asked by real people. The objections raised are real objections.

About the contents of this book

Firstly, it is incomplete. There are many objections and problems which I have not attempted to tackle. It has been difficult to decide what to include and what to leave out. Several pages of typing have ended in the wastepaper basket – very painful for an author! But I have had to draw the line somewhere, for this is intended to be an inexpensive paperback – not a definitive statement on every issue under the sun.

Secondly, this book is based on an earlier book with the same title. Some chapters are fairly similar in both editions. But I have reworked the whole book, and added a lot of new material. The earlier book had twelve chapters and few jokes. This book has twenty-one chapters (some of them very short) and six pages of attempted jokes. So –

whether or not you have a copy of the earlier edition – I hope you will read this new book, pass it to a friend, and persuade a church leader to use it for discussion groups. But I readily admit to extreme bias in this matter.

Thirdly, the book has a pattern. In particular, an argument is developed from section to section in the second half of the book. However, each chapter is self-contained and some subjects are more difficult than others. So I don't mind in the least if you pick out the chapters which interest you most – although I hope that you will read the entire book eventually.

About the title
Recently, I listened to a discussion entitled "Why I Remain a Christian". It was a good title, demanding thoughtful responses from a group of intelligent, sensitive people.

They had read a fair bit of history, and they knew about the atrocities of the Crusades, and the tortures of the Inquisition. They knew, too, that many powerful minds have argued against the Christian Faith. And they had long experience of church membership – they knew from personal experience about the pettiness, blindness and prejudice which sometimes spoils church life.

Yet they continued to believe. Despite all the problems, their faith in God as Love, and Jesus Christ as Lord, remained unshaken.

Shortly after that, I spent a discussion weekend with a group of students. We invited John Polkinghorne to lead us. He is a Fellow of the Royal Society, and until recently he was Professor of Mathematical Physics at Cambridge University. Then in his forties, John believed that God was calling him to full-time ministry within the Church. At the same time, his wife Ruth – also a mathematician – started to train as a nurse.

After his ordination in 1982 they went to live in a parish in Bristol, where John served as a curate. He finds that his scientific understanding *strengthens* his faith in God. He does not have a split personality – half scientist, half Christian. Despite his change of career, he has not turned his back on science. It is John's conviction that God is concerned with *every* aspect of life – not just with religion.

What is it that keeps such people within the Christian Church? This book is an attempt to answer that question. It is written in the knowledge that many important objections continue to be raised against the Christian Faith. It is written in the conviction that – despite these objections – Christianity is true. It is an attempt to act as counsel for the defence in "The Case Against Christ".

About you, the reader
I hope that atheists and agnostics will read this book – especially those who have always assumed that Christianity is a fairy-tale. The fact that several clever, well-balanced people are active Christians – people like those I have just described – does not prove that Christianity is true. But it does suggest *that it is worth investigating*. That is all I ask.

Most people who read this book won't be convinced atheists. It is much more likely that they will be "half-way to faith" – interested in, but unconvinced about, Christianity. More than anyone else, it is for them that I am writing, for I once stood where they stand, and I understand their problems "from the inside".

If this revised and expanded edition of *The Case Against Christ* fares like the first edition, it will also be read by many Christians who are sensitive to three facts. Firstly, that attacks are often made on their faith by people who hold different views. Secondly, that they sometimes lack the information needed to cope with such attacks. Thirdly, that Christianity is often regarded with a good-natured indifference – which can be harder to cope with than outright criticism.

Objections to Christianity are not new, of course. One of the earliest problems for Christians was the accusation that they were cannibals, because they spoke of "feeding on

Christ" in Holy Communion! Centuries later (in 1736), Bishop Butler complained that "many persons" assume that the Christian Faith is fictitious – suitable only for "mirth and ridicule".

It is necessary to think through the different challenges presented in every generation, and I hope that this book might encourage my fellow Christians in their efforts to do this.

To this end, I shall discuss many questions, debate many issues, and develop many arguments. But throughout I have been haunted by one short sentence – spoken, I think, by Martin Buber, a great Jewish teacher of our century. Concerning belief in God, "there are no *evidences*; there are only *witnesses*."

Strictly speaking, this is not true. Certainly there are no knock-down, totally watertight arguments which prove the existence of God. But there are sound reasons for belief, based on accurate, detailed information.

However, most of these reasons come to us in human shape. It is *people* who befriend us, teach us, love us, convince us, nurture us. It is our fellow human beings who share their beliefs, convictions and experiences with us, and point us to their source of strength and inspiration.

I have been greatly privileged to meet, and to read books by, many such witnesses – impressive men, women and young people who ring true. In what follows, I shall draw on them frequently. In one sense this is a book about them, as much as it is about the truths of which they have convinced me.

CONCLUDING QUOTATION

Christianity is a statement which, if false, is of *no* importance, and, if true, of infinite importance. The one thing it cannot be is moderately important – *C. S. Lewis.*

Part I

Questions: mainly about the Church

Organised Christianity has probably done more to retard the ideals that were its founders than any other agency in the world.

Richard le Gallienne

He cannot have God for his father who has not the Church for his mother.

St. Cyprian

We have been dosing our people with religion, when what they want is not this but the living God.

Frederick Denison Maurice

2

IN BRIEF

Many of the objections we shall examine will require at least one complete chapter, but we shall start by looking at six problems which can be considered rather more briefly.

1. It doesn't matter what you believe, as long as you are sincere

"It doesn't matter what you believe provided you live a good life. Sincerity counts more than anything else. It is what you *do* that matters, not what you believe."

Statements like this are common when people discuss religion. The trouble is that they oversimplify, for beliefs and actions are tied up together.

If you believe that the gods are pleased by human sacrifice, then it is tough on your children. If your witch doctor believes that a hole bored in your head will cure headaches, it is tough on you. If the terrorist who hijacks your plane sincerely believes in his cause, you are in for a rough time.

We are right to value sincerity, but false beliefs – even sincerely held false beliefs – can be disastrous. Indeed, the more sincere your "doctor" is about boring a hole in your head, the worse it will be. And the most sincere terrorist is the most dangerous of all.

Belief governs action.

Why was it that the Nazis caused such havoc in Europe? It was because they *believed* that the German people were a super-race, with a destiny to rule the world. Why did the American government cause such suffering by dropping an atomic bomb on Hiroshima on 6th August, 1945? It was because they *believed* that this would shorten the war (or that it would "impress" the Russians, depending on your view of history).

This connection between faith and action applies to everything. It is what a person *believes* that makes him an atheist, or a Buddhist, or a Christian, or a Communist – or a terrorist.

The most brilliant scientist cannot get a government post until he has been security checked. They want to know what he believes. Until they know this, he is regarded as a risk. It is because of the strong link between belief and behaviour that some regimes go in for brainwashing.

Our beliefs are vitally important.

2. Religion is dull

If someone at a wedding drinks lemonade, believing it to be champagne, she may think that champagne is dull. But she will be wrong, for she is passing judgment on the wrong thing.

Most people have had some experience of "religion". And they have found it boring. The lack of enthusiasm in the singing, the lack of warmth in the welcome, the constant appeals for funds – things like this have put them off. On the other hand, fewer people have experienced living, vital, Christianity. But because of their experience of religion, many people dismiss Christianity, for they think these are the same thing.

It is rather like a vaccination. You can be prevented from catching the real thing, by a smaller dose of something similar.

The actor Paul Jones played a leading role in the recent revival of *Guys and Dolls* in London's West End. He was put off religion at school. Some school religion is good, but in his case the stress was entirely on *duty*. There was no joy. It was boring and unrelated to his life. Many years later he came to a living faith in Christ, and experienced a new quality of life. He began to understand the words of Jesus: "I have come that they may have life, and have it to the full" (John 10:10).

Religion can be deadly dull. It is Christ who brings it to life. *He* can transform religion into vital, adventurous faith. When he does so, the outward expressions of that faith – worship, prayer, Bible reading, fellowship – come to life as well.

There is all the difference in the world between formal religion and real Christianity. Mind you, we are forbidden by Jesus to attempt to decide whose religion is formal, and whose is really alive. To start judging other people in this way is a very slippery slope indeed. *We* can't tell; only God can.

Closely related to this objection is the view that Christianity is irrelevant. The central Christian claim tackles this head-on. We believe that Jesus Christ is alive and active in our world. If we will allow him to do so, he will guide us, inspire us, strengthen and transform us.

This is not just theory. I think of a rather lonely young man who was drifting aimlessly, whose life is now full of purpose and friends. I think of a vicious criminal who left prison and worked hard to support other people in need.

Why the change? Each of them speaks of the power of Christ in his life. In this book I shall introduce you to many people whose lives have been deeply influenced in the same way, and for the same reason. You must decide for yourself whether or not they are deluded.

3. A bad case of wishful thinking

At Christmas, the churches are crowded. People flock in to sing the familiar carols; to see the candlelit churches; to watch the children's Nativity plays. It's all very magical – and I love it!

For some people, Christmas means a large dose of wistful, wishful thinking. If only . . . if only it could be true. But all that talk about heavenly choirs and guiding stars takes a bit of believing. And it isn't too difficult to think of an alternative explanation for the too-early pregnancy of an attractive young woman.

So let's brighten up our lives for an hour or two. Let's pretend – but not for too long. Boxing Day will soon be here – and endless turkey soup to remind us that Christmas is just an interlude.

Wishful thinking is a real danger. We want something to be true, so we convince ourselves that it *is* true. Perhaps Christians are those who never get back to reality. Perhaps Christianity is a case of pretending that Boxing Day will never come.

Perhaps . . . but the trouble with that line of reasoning is that it works in two directions.

Aldous Huxley, author of *Brave New World* and many other books, admitted that for many years he asserted his atheism for just this reason. The idea of God was extremely *in*convenient. He didn't want the world to have any long-term meaning, because he wanted to live without irksome moral controls. So he chose to believe that God does not exist, and that the world has no meaning. Later in life, he was honest enough to admit his motives for believing this.

No doubt there are Christians who desperately want the

Christian Faith to be true – perhaps because they are afraid of death, or for some other reason. But as we have seen, there are non-Christians who would greatly prefer that it wasn't true. And many Christians often wish that the way of Christ wasn't so demanding.

The assertion that "it's all wishful thinking" can work for and against Christianity. It leaves untouched the really central question: yes, but is it *true* or *false*?

This is an appropriate point to say a word about the famous "placebo effect" (you take aspirin and your headache disappears. I take what *I think* is aspirin, and my headache disappears). This is sometimes applied to religion by its critics who say: Christianity works for you because *you believe it to be true*, not because it *is* true.

Perhaps. Perhaps not. Certainly the placebo effect is a reality – in medicine at least. In trials, more than one-third of those who were given what they thought was morphine (but wasn't) reported a reduction in pain. But this leaves about 60 per cent for whom belief without substance *didn't* work.

I would estimate that the same kind of figure might apply to a religion without any basis in fact and reality. The placebo effect seems to be clearest in neurotic subjects. Again, while some Christians are mentally unstable, many others are very well balanced indeed.

4. You don't need to go to church to be a Christian

If this statement means that you can be a nice person without going to church, then it is obviously true. But if it means that you can be a follower of Jesus Christ without joining a church, the assertion is rather more problematic.

For one thing, the word disciple means "learner". If we really do want to learn about the way of Jesus, then church isn't a bad place to start. But there is another reason too. Jesus chose twelve men and he taught them as a group. From that moment on, his followers had to learn to get on with each other – and it wasn't always easy.

He made it clear that they must work *together*. Like it or not, they were to think of themselves as a community and as a family. In some families, various members don't meet together, nor speak to one another. When this happens, we know that things have gone wrong. The same is true of the Church – the family of God.

Behind this common objection, there is another assumption too – the assumption that worship isn't very important. I would want to argue with that as well. At first sight it doesn't seem to have much to do with the real world – but first impressions can be wrong. Worship isn't a hobby for those who like singing hymns; it is more serious than that.

In worship we are *admitting* something important about ourselves – that we are dependent upon one another and upon God, and that we need his forgiveness and grace. Even more important, in worship we are *doing* something about the state of the world – at least, that is the Christian claim.

Archbishop Michael Ramsey told a pointed parable. It concerns a man with boils, who visited his doctor. The doctor told his patient that he couldn't treat the boils, without treating the poison in his body. The same is true of the human race. We have several nasty boils in the social and moral order: the build-up of weapons; antagonism between different races; the great gap between rich and poor.

To deal with them properly, we need to go to the root, and to deal with the poison in the system. Michael Ramsey concludes that worship helps us to deal with that poison: "The root is the right relation of man to Creator: and when Christians are concerned about what they call worship they are concerned, not with something remote or escapist, but with the root of the world's predicament."

5. God was an astronaut!

We live in a scientific age, but belief in powers and forces which science cannot explain remains strong. Astrology is amazingly popular, and horoscopes abound. For many people this is "just a bit of fun". Others – some of them highly educated – take it very seriously indeed.

Astrology is only one aspect. On holiday I visited a small library in Sussex. The "Religious Books" section was light on serious theology, but heavy on sensation, and on such subjects as spiritualism and ESP (extra-sensory perception – telepathy, etc.). Three large books probed the question: was God an astronaut? The date-stamp pages indicated high popularity.

It is clear that modern man has not "come of age" after all. We mix our scientific view of the world with a large dose of superstition and credulity.

I thought hard about tackling some of these issues in this book, but it became clear that *general* arguments would not do. Each piece of evidence (or "evidence") needs to be examined carefully, and that would take too much space. So, with some reluctance, I have left these problems on one side. But I will make two observations.

Firstly, a word to those who are interested in the "was God an astronaut?" question. This has been popularised by Erich von Daniken in a whole series of books. These have sold in vast numbers and I salute him as a fine – and highly imaginative! – communicator. But I don't know of a single expert in the fields which he covers who lends any support to his views.

If this subject interests you, I suggest you read *Some Trust in Chariots* edited by E. W. Castle and B. B. Thiering. The book contains chapters by sixteen experts whose personal beliefs range from Christian to agnostic. Between them they cover a variety of specialisms from ancient history to modern engineering. The engineer examines in detail some of von Daniken's claims and speaks for the other contributors when he says: "It seems fatuous of Herr von Daniken to have built such an extensive theory on such readily disprovable premises. He should have done his homework better!"

Sadly, Castle's book is out of print, but it is available from libraries.

Secondly, we must not lump all these fringe subjects together. For example, ESP is an important area of study, requiring careful research. As for astrology – the most popular of all – I will risk unpopularity by advising people who dabble in this to leave it alone. The Christian Faith does not encourage us to peer into the future. Instead, it encourages us to face the future with trust and confidence in the living God. People who have future events in their lives "revealed" to them by horoscopes or fortune-tellers, often tend (unconsciously) to let this information shape their lives.

6. Christianity is humourless

At first sight – and perhaps at second sight, too – this appears to be the case. Exuberance and joy have an obvious place in a faith which celebrates resurrection and life. But worship varies in mood. As we keep watch with Jesus in Gethsemane we are quiet and still. As we consider Calvary we are solemn and serious. Perhaps we shall be moved to tears.

The same is true of the Bible. Jesus encourages those who mourn, "for they will be comforted". St. James bids us to "grieve, mourn and wail". Tears are not out of place as we consider the spiritual poverty of our lives, the bitter divisions in our world, and the cost of our redemption.

This is not the whole story though. Overall, the New Testament is a happy book. Read it, and a range of positive words stand out: joy, rejoice, blessed (which means happy). And there are jokes in the New Testament. Some of these are puns which don't translate well from the Greek. Some of them have been blunted by familiarity.

I am quite sure that Jesus' teaching would often have raised a smile – and probably a guffaw or two. A camel trying to get through the eye of a needle, or a man with a plank in his eye (as opposed to a speck of sawdust), would not be out of place on the Goon Show or in a Lenny Henry sketch.

So if I need weighty justification for including a few jokes in this book, that would be it. But perhaps I need no deeper excuse than to say that I enjoy jokes, and that you, dear reader (as a Victorian author might say), may well need a break from serious reading from time to time. If you find that a chapter gets tough, or if your eyes begin to close, turn to a page entitled *Take a Break*!

* * *

We have looked at some of the objections which are raised against Christianity, and we shall be considering several more. This may give the impression of a defensive "back to the wall" attitude.

In fact, of course, Christians are not alone in facing problems raised by their beliefs. For example, a group of agnostics published a book entitled *Objections to Humanism*, in which they spoke of the difficulties which *they* face as a result of *their* beliefs.

Every view of life raises problems, and it is important that they should be faced and discussed, not ignored or buried.

TAKE A BREAK (1)
A LITTLE CHILD SHALL LEAD THEM

When church services are too long
The church service was far too long for Billy aged seven. He looked around for interesting distractions. "What's that?" he asked, pointing to the names on the roll of honour, affixed to the wall. "Those are the people who died in the Services," whispered his mother. "Oh," said Billy, intrigued, "did they die in the morning services or the evening services?"

* * *

When the truth is too hard to bear
A primary school youngster was asked to write about the summer holidays. She showed her composition to Mum. "Our Mary didn't go to Africa!" protested Mum. "She went to Gloucester." "I know," said Jane, "but I couldn't spell Gloucester."

*   *   *

A shepherd to his flock
A young boy sat near the front at the Confirmation Service. He was intrigued by the shepherd's crook which the bishop carried. At Sunday School the following week he was asked to write about the Confirmation. He wrote: "Last Sunday I sat near the bishop. Now I know what a crook looks like."

*   *   *

A true story
We attended a modern pantomime based on the Nativity story. King Herod stormed about the stage, looking for little boys and ranting "Fe, fi, fo, fum. I smell the blood of an Englishman." Suddenly he stopped. "Ah, ha," he shouted. "I smell a little boy." There was a pause. Then a little voice from the front row called out indignantly, "Well, it wasn't me!"

*   *   *

Rewriting history
They were casting the school Nativity Play. Michael badly wanted to play one of the central figures. But he and his teacher didn't always get on too well, so he was given a safe minor part as the innkeeper. "I'll learn her," muttered Michael to himself. After many hitchless rehearsals, the big day came. The hall was packed with parents, teachers and governors. Along came the Holy Family. "Is there any room in the inn?" asked Joseph. Michael grinned and threw open the doors. "Plenty of room," he replied. "Come on in."

POSTSCRIPT ON BRAINWASHING

Some religious sects brainwash people into their ways and beliefs. Aware of this danger, when I taught Religious Education, I was concerned to *educate*, not *indoctrinate*, my pupils. I wanted them to think for themselves, not simply to accept my views second hand.

In my clearer moments, I realised how absurd I was to worry about indoctrinating those children in an hour per week – for many of them were thoroughly brainwashed already!

Some were indoctrinated by the ad-man; they believed that happiness came from piling up possessions. Others were brainwashed into believing that religion is irrelevant to life. They didn't *think* about these things: they simply took them for granted.

The same is true of many adults, too. In inviting unbelievers to read this book, I am being cheeky. For I am asking them to acknowledge that their present views about Christianity may not result from hard thought – but from prejudice, or from inadequate information, or from a second-hand acceptance of other people's opinions and attitudes.

I hope that they will forgive my boldness, which arises from my own experience. For that was my position with regard to the Christian Faith for many years – and I sadly confess that it remains my position in some areas of life, even now.

3

THOSE HYPOCRITICAL CHRISTIANS!

In York – the city in which I live – there is a famous medieval street called the Shambles. Old buildings lean across a narrow cobbled road. If you lean out of one upstairs window, you can touch the house opposite. It is very picturesque, and a "must" for tourists.

One house in the street was the home of Margaret Clitherow – a devout Roman Catholic who lived in the sixteenth century. Accused of harbouring priests, she refused to plead her case – in order to save her children from being forced to witness against her.

As a result she was crushed to death by heavy weights, on the orders of a "Christian" state. That terrible incident reminds us that anyone who tries to defend the record of the Christian Church has a tough job.

Christian history is very mixed. There have been plenty of saints; there has been a great deal of courage; there has been a lot of love. But only a fool would pretend that this tells the whole story. Christian history is blackened by the execution of innocent people because they were Protestant or Catholic; by the enforced "conversion" of whole populations; by the unwillingness of many in the Church to fight against social evils. And I frequently talk with people who say that they don't attend church because they don't like the people who do! Words like "unfriendly", "clique" and "hypocrite" often come into such conversations.

Jesus was once asked to state the greatest commandment. In reply, he summarised the Old Testament Law: Love God with all your strength, and love your neighbour as yourself. This is crystal clear. Why then has the Church so often strayed so far from his teaching? I will offer three reasons.

1. Non-Christian leaders in the Church

When the Church became very powerful, it was invaded by ambition. Men with little regard for the teaching of Christ, and far from the Spirit of Christ, held high positions within the Church of Christ. Their concern was not to follow Jesus of Nazareth, but to gain power, prestige or wealth.

Perhaps this was inevitable during those centuries when everyone in Europe who was not a Jew or a Muslim was automatically regarded as a Christian. Which brings us to the second reason:

2. Elastic use of the word Christian

Over the years, the word "Christian" has been stretched in

two directions. *On the one hand* it is often used as a compliment. I remember hearing someone describe his friend as a Communist and an atheist. He added, "but he's as good a Christian as you or me." He wanted to say that he thought his friend was a good man, so he used the word "Christian".

If he was using the word correctly, then it would be intolerable for anyone to say "I am a Christian." That would be the worst kind of boasting. But the follower of Christ does not mean "I am a specially good person" when he claims to be a Christian.

It is easy to see how the word came to be used in this way. Followers of Jesus are expected to lead good lives. But to apply this word to all people whom we admire, whether or not they follow Jesus Christ, simply causes confusion. After all, his name makes up two-thirds of the word. Besides, it is unfair to a large number of atheists and agnostics to saddle them with a word they don't want.

The word "Christian" began its life in the New Testament, and it is used there, not as a compliment, but as a *description*. It describes a person who believes that Jesus Christ is the Son of God, and who – often unsuccessfully – tries to follow and worship him.

This is the way in which the word is used throughout this book. When I call a person a non-Christian, I am not intending to insult him. Nor am I suggesting that he is inferior to the person who is a Christian. The phrase is used simply to record the fact that he does not acknowledge Jesus Christ as his Lord and Saviour.

On the other hand, the word "Christian" has been watered down. Far from being used as a compliment, or referring to an individual committed to the way of Christ, it is often applied to almost anyone who was born in a "Christian country".

The problem continues today. A wry story from Northern Ireland tells of a young man who was asked whether he was Catholic or Protestant. "I'm not a Christian," he

replied. "I'm an agnostic. But I'm a Protestant agnostic"!
This illustrates all too clearly the muddle over words
produced by centuries of Christian history.

The problem is even more acute in the Middle East. We
read in the newspapers of whole groups of "Christian"
soldiers. Sometimes they commit terrible acts of violence.
Possibly, some of these soldiers are Christian in a deeper
sense. But most of them aren't. The word "Christian" is
used as a convenience – to distinguish them from other
groups, such as Muslims and Jews.

3. Christians are sinners

Convenient as it would be, we can't blame *all* the bad things
in the Church onto people who aren't really Christian at all.
Christians are sinners, and they share much of the prejudice and ignorance of the age in which they live. No doubt
many soldiers in the Crusades were devout men who
sincerely believed in their cause. From our viewpoint, they
were sincerely wrong.

So the objection remains. Christians are *not* good
people. However, there is one saving factor. They *know*
they are not, and it is for this very reason that they find
Jesus Christ so important.

Jesus is not just a great teacher, or a fine example. In the
Bible he is called a *Saviour*. The word means "Saver" or
"Rescuer". He rescues people from their selfishness, their
indifference to the needs of others, their pride, their
jealousy, their snobbishness, their lust – those things which
spoil our lives, and which sometimes make us ashamed.

Jesus spoke of himself as a doctor. "It is not the healthy
who need a doctor, but the sick," he said. "I have not come
to call the righteous, but sinners" (Mark 2:17). Christians
are sinners who have responded to this invitation.

When Christians go to church, they are not trying to
impress other people with their uprightness and goodness.
This would be like going to hospital to show how healthy
you are!

One of the most important aspects of any church service is the confession of our sins. We publicly acknowledge our moral and spiritual poverty – and we ask for God's forgiveness and strength. Each church is like an outpatients' department in a hospital for the spiritually and morally sick.

In some ways the marvel is, not that the Church fails so often, but that it has done any good at all. For it is made up of self-confessed moral failures.

Christians are not basically good, respectable people. They are thoroughly dissatisfied people. They are dissatisfied with *themselves*. They know that they are selfish; or that they cannot control their tempers; or that they are jealous; or greedy; or lazy; or . . . It is because they know their own shortcomings, and their own great needs, that they have gone to the one Person who can help them: Jesus Christ, the Great Physician.

But sometimes a cure takes a long time. Especially when someone has a really bad dose of an illness. Sometimes the protest that "Christians are no better than anyone else" is not true, because it does not go far enough. Some Christians are a lot *worse*, by ordinary standards.

For example, there are criminals, drug addicts, and alcoholics who are real Christians. Their lives are not always changed in an instant. But because a cure ultimately depends on the power of Christ, and not on the individual Christian, a successful outcome is certain in the long run.

The disease of sin, no matter how severe, will always be healed eventually, if the person puts himself into Christ's hands. The trouble is, that we all have something wrong with us, and an apparently mild attack will get steadily worse, if it is not treated.

POSTSCRIPT ON SIN AND GUILT

This book has hardly begun, and already we are deep into talk about sin. Sure confirmation that the Church is too concerned with sin and guilt!

In fact, you won't find much more about these particular subjects in this book, but it is worth spending a few paragraphs looking at this particular objection. Perhaps it was best summed up by the parishioner who complained: "Until our new vicar arrived, we didn't know what sin was"!

First, a word about guilt. This has had a bad press from some psychologists, and it is often assumed that guilt feelings are always bad. Of course, vague, unfocussed feelings of guilt are unhealthy. But a sense of guilt isn't always a bad thing. If I steal your wallet, your wife, or your reputation, I am guilty, and there is only hope for me – and for you – if I *feel guilty*. A psychopath would feel no guilt; a healthy person would feel lots. But guilt needs to be put to work. If it doesn't lead to repentance and restoration, it is useless.

Secondly, let's turn our attention to sin. The most important point to notice is that Christianity isn't in the least interested in sin. It is intensely interested in the *forgiveness* of sins, and *liberation* from sin's power – which is a different matter altogether.

Sin can be defined in various ways. The simplest way is to think of it as breaking God's law. Looked at like this, most people are against sin. Read the Ten Commandments (Exod. 20) and you will probably agree with most of them. For most of us are against being killed, or having our property stolen, or our reputation damaged.

Another way of defining sin is as self-centredness. Most of us are against this too – in other people at least. Think of a totally selfish character in a TV soap opera – someone whose whole life is centred on him/herself and whose ambitions take no account of other people's feelings.

Christianity is against that approach to life, because it is intensely damaging – to the person who lives like that, and to the people with whom he lives and works. In the end, lives that are lived in that way become sad and empty. In saying that the Church is against this approach to life, we are saying that Christ is *for* their opposites. He stands for thoughtfulness, kindness, forgiveness, co-operation, openness, and generosity.

To some extent, all of us are like the selfish character in the TV series. We all settle too easily for a comfortable life, and we don't fight, give, or pray hard enough for other people's rights and happiness. So we mustn't point the finger too readily – except at ourselves, perhaps. We *all* need to be challenged, inspired and strengthened if we are to get a wider vision, and a bigger heart.

Which is where Jesus comes in. He came to deal with sin and to remove guilt. To put this another way: he wants to free us from fear, anxiety and self-centredness, so that we can live in joy, peace and love.

This is summed up very powerfully by Harry Williams, an Anglican monk who was Prince Charles' tutor at Cambridge, and who read a lesson at his wedding: "Being a Christian means . . . being people in whom his (Jesus') life and character and power are manifest and energised . . . Christian experience is not so much a matter of imitating a leader . . . as accepting and receiving a new quality of life – a life infinitely more profound and dynamic and meaningful than human life without Christ.'

4

THE CREDIT SIDE

If we think about the Inquisition, and about the violent quarrels between some Roman Catholics and Protestants in Northern Ireland, we shall – alas – be thinking about facts. If we concentrate on the dullness of many church services, the constant begging for money, and the refusal of many church-goers to "get involved" we shall, sadly, be thinking about more facts. But not *all* the facts.

If Jesus Christ really *does* help his followers to overcome their selfishness, and if he really *does* pour his love into their lives, we should expect to find some practical evidence of this. We are not disappointed. There *is* a credit side.

The failures are great, but the successes are tremendous too.

Christianity certainly has no monopoly on love, goodness and social action. But enough men and women have done great things *because* of their Christian faith, to show that the accusation that Christians are unfriendly, uninvolved, or hypocritical, is not always true. Here are a few examples, taken from the early days of the Church, from the Victorian Church, and from our own times.

1. The Early Church
The early Christians were impressive. In one sense they were very ordinary, and they failed a great deal. The fact remains that they "conquered" the brutal, well-organised, Roman Empire. They captured it for Jesus Christ and for his gospel of love, with a single weapon – the quality of their lives. They showed love in a world which valued indifference. They demonstrated joy and deep happiness in a world where people settled for pleasure. They practised forgiveness in a world which believed in harsh revenge.

Early in the fourth century, the Christian Faith had become the official religion of the Roman Empire – with very mixed blessings for that Faith. Later in that same century the anti-Christian Emperor Julian came to the throne. He accused the Christians of atheism because they believed in one invisible God – and a God who could not be seen or touched was no God at all! He was determined to reinstate the pagan gods. Julian lost his crusade, and he was honest enough to say why. His words are impressive because he was an opponent of the Christian way.

"Atheism (i.e. Christian Faith) has been specially advanced through the loving service rendered to strangers, and through their care for the burial of the dead. It is a scandal that there is not a single Jew who is a beggar, and that the godless Galileans care not only for their own poor but for ours as well; while those who belong to us look in vain for the help that we should render them."

The "loving service" of the early Christians challenged and changed deep-seated attitudes. Antony Bridge, a convert from atheism who became Dean of Guildford, preached a powerful sermon in which he asked: why value love at all? He went on to admit that this sounds like an idiotic question, because most of us assume that love is a virtue. Then he made an important contrast:

"But other civilisations have assumed no such thing. Courage, stoic endurance, the search for wisdom, intellectual integrity, strength, detachment – these are the virtues normally worshipped by mankind and preached by his many religions. And love is a contradiction of many of them."

Despite this, most of us continue to believe in love – even if we don't always practise it. We do so because of thousands of years of teaching by Jews and Christians – and because love is emphasised by modern psychologists. That was Antony Bridge's conclusion.

2. Yesterday's Church

The Church of the last century is often criticised. It is too easily assumed that nineteenth-century Christians were universally hypocritical – praying in their churches on Sunday, and exploiting in their factories on Monday. Sadly, there were – and are – hypocrites in the Church, but this view does not express the whole truth.

For one thing, there were many working-class Christians. It is tragically true that the Church lost touch with many workers during the Industrial Revolution. But not with all workers. Indeed, Christianity played a central role in the struggle by British workers to form trades' unions.

In 1830, Dorset farm labourers earned nine shillings a week. By 1834 this had been reduced to seven shillings, with the threat of a further one-shilling reduction. With George Loveless as their leader, and the Vicar of

Tolpuddle as an intermediary, the men tried to negotiate with their employers. Promises were made but not kept. Eventually the men formed a union – the Friendly Society of Agricultural Labourers – for which six of them were sentenced to deportation. Five of these "Tolpuddle Martyrs" were Methodists. The Loveless brothers were local preachers. Their ability to organise and to speak in public grew out of their Christian roots.

The famous . . . The involvement of some Victorian Christians in crusades *against* grinding poverty and *for* social reform is legendary. Societies founded then continue to be honoured throughout the world.

Foremost among these are organisations for children: the National Children's Home (a Methodist Foundation), Spurgeon's Homes (a Baptist Foundation), Muller's Homes (Evangelical Brethren), the Children's Society (Anglican). And excellent work is done in the many local authority homes which grew from this Christian soil.

The most famous individual in this field is "Dr." Barnardo with his motto, written in brick: "No destitute child ever refused admission". It was a heroic promise, given the large number of homeless children in London. The motto itself resulted from tragedy. A boy called "Carrots" was given money and told to return later, because the home was full. He did not return, for he died of exposure.

Yet London nearly lost Barnardo to China, for he seriously considered missionary work. The movement which he started has spread to many countries around the world.

In his book *Civilisation*, Lord Clark – not himself a Christian – wrote about the Quaker Elizabeth Fry, whose "spiritual influence on the prisoners at Newgate was really a miracle". He went on to pay tribute to William Wilberforce and Lord Shaftesbury. For their struggles against slavery, and for a host of social reforms, he described them as two of the greatest names "in the history of humanitarianism".

Each met fierce opposition, each based his life and work on the Bible, and each found support from other Christian leaders. For example, one week before he died, John Wesley – founder of Methodism – wrote to Wilberforce. It was probably his last letter: "Go on in the name of God and in the power of his might, till even American slavery (the vilest that ever saw the sun) shall vanish away before it."

Then there were the Christian Socialists. Men like Charles Kingsley, the Anglican clergyman whose *Water Babies* focussed on the plight of chimney boys. Women like Margaret MacMillan whose vision and energy helped to revolutionise education. She insisted that schools should be happy places. She introduced nursery schools, swimming pools, and school meals into Bradford, where rickets was common.

Her ideas fired other imaginations, and her influence continues today. In Parliament in 1944 she was described as "the greatest educationist this country ever produced". J. B. Priestley gave a typically passionate, gritty accolade: "Such persons, single-minded, pure in heart, blazing with selfless love, are the jewels of our species . . . if it were not for them, plus a few glorious artists, this world would be one huge ashpit."

. . . and the less famous: Barnardo, Wilberforce and Elizabeth Fry are well known. But who has heard of R. W. Lowry? On 13th November, 1885, the *Church Times* published a letter in which he asked for support for a home established by "two ladies . . . with the warm approval of the Bishop of the Diocese".

The home was for twelve young girls who had been rescued from child prostitution – a work paralleled in our own century by Father Joe Williamson of Stepney. The women wanted to take in many more children, and to help them, "till the children are able to help themselves". No doubt many others – like R. W. Lowry and the "two ladies" – did their work with little recognition, and with no subsequent fame.

Limitations: The work of these reformers can be criticised. Each of them had limitations and prejudices – especially when judged by twentieth-century eyes. The fact remains that the energy, vision and compassion which sprang from their faith in Christ improved the quality of life for millions.

Their labours were sometimes warmly appreciated. At Shaftesbury's funeral in October 1885, thousands lined the streets – some of the factory workers, miners, chimney boys, ragged children (Shaftesbury knew and helped Barnardo), flower girls, farm workers, "lunatics" and criminals who had benefited from his reforms.

A poignant cry went up: "Our Earl's gone." Shaftesbury Avenue and Piccadilly's "Eros" are his memorials in brick, metal and stone. His greater memorial is thousands of lives touched by his love and energy.

Outside Britain: Britain had no monopoly on compassion. Father Damien, a Belgian priest, volunteered for work among leprosy sufferers who were treated as outcasts. His inspiring work on the Hawaiian island of Molokai involved building houses, and providing a water supply, in addition to elementary medical care. He contracted leprosy himself in 1885, and died in 1889, at the age of 49.

Since then enormous progress has been made, much of it pioneered by Christians – both missionaries and nationals. Mary Verghese, Paul Brand and Stanley Browne come to mind. When the latter was awarded the Royal African Society's medal in 1970, the Council spoke of his "unrivalled knowledge of leprosy research and control".

The task is still enormous. Of an estimated fifteen million

leprosy sufferers, only three million are receiving treatment. But this brings us to the present day, and to our final section in this chapter.

3. Today's Church

A story is told about an English archbishop who visited America. On arrival he held a news conference. *Question*: will you be visiting a night club in New York? *Clever answer*: *are* there any night clubs in New York? *Headlines in newspaper*: Archbishop's first question – are there any night clubs in New York?

He was putty in their hands. This is one view of the Church strongly pressed on television. Christian leaders are shown as innocents abroad – humble do-gooders, who do no good. The success of Terry Waite's patient diplomacy in obtaining release for hostages has drawn the sting a little, but the image persists.

Off the television screen, comments are sometimes harsher. In our college chapel we have a board for prayer requests. Slips of paper are provided which start *Please pray for* . . . One morning I found the following "request". *Please pray for* . . . "All Christians, that they may become less sanctimonious . . ." Painfully, I realised how we Christians appear to some people who don't share our faith.

But despite its weak television image, and despite its many failures, the Church this century continues to be impressive in many ways.

Resisting evil: When Hitler came to power in Germany, he tried to use the Church to gain support. To their shame, some churchmen agreed, not seeing the monstrous shape of things to come. But some refused to co-operate. They formed the "Confessing Church" in Germany, and throughout the entire period of Hitler's power, they opposed him. E. H. Robertson, an expert on the Church in Germany during the war period, wrote:

The resistance of the Confessing Church to the policy of Hitler continued into and through the war years. It also survived the bitter attack on all opposition and non-conformity, and raised its voice constantly in 2,000 pulpits and in every possible way.

Black Church leaders spearheaded the struggle for civil rights in the USA in the 1960s. This movement was led from the front by Martin Luther King, a Baptist pastor, who – following Gandhi – advocated non-violent resistance. He preached a sermon entitled "A Tough Mind and a Tender Heart". These seven words sum him up.

After his assassination on 4th April, 1968, one black man went into the streets to shoot the first white man he met. Martin Luther King would have regarded this as a total failure for his message. In contrast he would have drawn encouragement from his wife Coretta. As she discussed her husband's murder with their children, she urged them not to hate the assassin.

As I write, a similar struggle dominates South Africa. Together with many others, I am appalled that the white South African leadership claims to be Christian. But I am also encouraged by the fine leadership shown by many black, coloured and white Christians in that troubled and divided land. Men and women like Dr. Allan Boesak, Mrs. Winnie Mandela ("a devout Anglican"), Rev. Nico Smith, Archbishop Desmond Tutu, the Nobel Peace Prize winner, and Dr. Beyers Naudé.

Many present-day leaders point to the tremendous influence upon them of Bishop Trevor Huddleston, and of Chief Albert Luthuli. The latter – a Christian Zulu leader – was awarded the Nobel Peace Prize twenty-five years ago. Whether the message of non-violent resistance preached by many of these leaders will win the hearts and wills of their oppressed neighbours is hard to predict.

Vision and commitment: Over the past few decades many caring and crusading agencies have sprung up. *Shelter* is one example. This organisation was formed on 1st December, 1966, in order to combat the enormous misery and suffering caused by the problem of homelessness in Britain.

It is not a specifically Christian organisation, but it finds a place here because Christians were prominent among those who set it up. This is clearly seen from the fact that Shelter resulted from the united concern of five organisations: the Notting Hill Housing Trust, the Catholic Housing Aid Society, the National Federation of Housing Associations, Christian Action, and the British Churches Housing Trust.

Of the five individuals singled out for special mention by Shelter in connection with the launching of the movement, three were Christian leaders. Bruce Kenrick, a Christian minister, was Shelter's first Chairman.

Samaritans is another example. Like Shelter, it is not a specifically Christian organisation. Regardless of their beliefs, men and women are invited to become helpers, provided they are willing to give their time, as listeners and befrienders. The phones are answered night and day, every day.

In Britain each year about 5,000 people commit suicide, and some 200,000 make an "unsuccessful" attempt. Many people believe that the Samaritans have played a key role in pegging numbers at this level. One thing is certain: their telephones and offices receive tens of thousands of callers each year.

The oak grew from an acorn. In 1953, a London rector became aware that a large number of people were suicidal and despairing. Chad Varah invited desperate people to ring Mansion House 9000. Within twenty years his simple idea had grown into an international movement.

Another burst of imaginative creative energy has resulted in the establishment of many hospices in Britain, over the past two decades. It was largely the vision and energy of far-sighted Christians which led to this. The work of the hospice movement in helping people to die with dignity is spreading. Recently, two hospices have been founded for children. The first of those – Helen House in Oxford – was established by Anglican nuns in 1982.

A great deal of good work is done in Christ's name, with little publicity – and little desire for publicity. Work with young people, centres for homeless men and women, communities for drug addicts and drop-outs, teas for elderly people, homes for handicapped people.

Jean Vanier is founder of l'Arche (the Ark) – a network of small communities providing love and care for mentally handicapped people. He summed up the driving force behind many individuals who give their spare time, or devote their lives, to these enterprises: "We all have to choose between two ways of being crazy: the foolishness of the Gospel and the nonsense of the values of our world".*

From many other areas which merit comment, I want to pay tribute to the work for peace of the Quakers and Brethren, and to the work on the "fringes" of society of the Church Army and the Salvation Army. One of the latter's numerous enterprises is a highly professional Missing Persons Bureau. For many years, they have regarded the fact that large numbers of people simply "disappear" as a human problem requiring specialist knowledge. Each year their Bureau helps restore nearly 5,000 people to lost relatives. Always, they observe the highest standards of confidentiality.

The local Church: The national and international organ-

---

*One reader expressed surprise that a Christian should say that the Gospel is "foolish". If in doubt, look up 1 Corinthians 1:25!

isations listed above make a direct impact upon thousands of people, week by week. It remains true that the Christian Faith is mediated to most people by their local churches. For despite the much-publicised decline in church attendance, the network of local churches continues to attract large numbers. It is still the case that more people are in churches on Sundays than in football stadiums on Saturdays – and that was true before 1985, the worst year ever for football.

The quality of church life is tremendously patchy. The conduct of some clergy is embarrassing – I think of the vicar who roundly scolded his Carol Service congregation for not attending church more often. I could understand their reluctance! And it is all too possible to go to church as a stranger, and to remain unwelcomed by a single member of the congregation.

At the other end of the spectrum are congregations with vision, warmth, energy and commitment. During college vacations I visit a wide range of churches, large and small. You will gather that I am a not-uncritical observer. But I can record with total honesty the fact that I am often impressed with the imagination, care, support and vitality which I find.

Recently I came across this small note in a parish magazine: "Saint Luke's exists to serve the people of Burton Stone Lane and the surrounding area in whatever way possible in Christ's name. The Vicar is available at all times – should help be needed. Do not hesitate to get in touch with him at any time of day or night."

The man who wrote that is often very stretched. He is chaplain to a hospital as well as vicar of a parish. Sometimes he is at the hospital late on Saturday night, before a busy Sunday. Yet he offers himself "at any time of day or night" – and he means it. Such commitment from the rather undistinguished-looking church on the corner is more common than many people suppose.

We must stop there with the list incomplete. I am far from suggesting that Christians have a monopoly on social concern and action. But I would pose this question. If there had been no Jesus Christ, and hence no Christian Church, would the world be any poorer?

Ask the workers of the last century; ask the homeless children; ask the slaves; ask those suffering from leprosy; ask the despairing; as the homeless; ask the oppressed; ask the dying; ask ordinary parishioners.

And then ask yourself.

TAKE A BREAK (2)
ALL ABOUT BISHOPS

Poor bishops! For the most part they are upright, intelligent men, who work very hard. Yet they are a favourite target for jokes, some of which – as you will see – are in rather poor taste! I thank Stuart Blanch – a retired archbishop – for not insisting that this page, or his Foreword, must go, and I ask all bishops, everywhere, to forgive me. Fortunately, this is their Christian duty!

* * *

The bishop arrived to preach at Evensong, and he was disappointed at the turn-out. Rather annoyed, he questioned the vicar. "Didn't you tell them I was coming?" "No, my Lord", replied the hapless man, "but somehow the word seems to have got round."

* * *

A bishop was invited to the church fête, and the vicar talked to him about preaching. "Next Sunday I want to preach on humility. Can you recommend a good book on the subject?" The bishop pulled himself up to his full height. "There is only one," he replied, "and I wrote it."

* * *

It was early in the morning when the bishop and the dean went to the cathedral. No one else was about, except the cleaner, brush in hand. "I am nothing; I am nothing; I am nothing," said the bishop, beating his breast. "I am nothing; I am nothing; I am nothing," said the dean, beating his breast. "I am nothing; I am nothing; I am nothing," said the cleaner, beating his breast. The bishop sidled up to the dean, pointed to the cleaner, and hissed: "Look who thinks he's nothing."

* * *

There was an orderly queue at the pearly gates, when suddenly there was a loud fanfare of trumpets, and a great commotion. The gates opened, and an archbishop was rushed through in a huge Rolls-Royce. A little man near the front of the queue complained: "It's just the same in heaven as it was on earth; favouritism for the famous." The angel on duty laughed. "You've got it wrong, I'm afraid. Every day we let in thousands of ordinary people like you. But this is a day for celebration. We haven't admitted an archbishop for 300 years!"

* * *

This one's true (the last one wasn't, I promise). A bishop was conducting a large Communion service, and the public address system was playing up. He tapped the microphone, and said, "There's something wrong with this mike." But it was working well, and the vast congregation thought that the service had started. With one voice, they responded: "And also with you."

Part II

Questions about Science

Man is nothing but:

FAT enough for seven bars of soap

IRON enough for one medium-size nail

SUGAR enough for seven cups of tea

LIME enough to whitewash one chicken coop

MAGNESIUM enough for one dose of salts

PHOSPHOROUS enough to tip two thousand two hundred matches

POTASH enough to explode one toy crane

SULPHUR enough to rid one dog of fleas

Professor C. E. M. Joad

God does not play dice.

Albert Einstein

5

"BUT SURELY, SIR, SCIENCE HAS DISPROVED GOD?"

The sentence which forms our chapter heading was addressed by a sixth-former to Professor Coulson, the late Oxford mathematician. The fact that the professor was not only a leading scientist, but also a Christian leader, was something which that student could not sort out. In suggesting that science and religion are opposed, he was speaking for a good many people.

In fact, the particular combination found in Dr. Coulson – scientist *and* Christian – has not been uncommon throughout the history of science.

Then . . . Many of the founders of modern science were men with a firm belief in God. Robert Boyle

(1627–1691) and Sir Isaac Newton (1642–1727) are good examples.

Robert Boyle is well known for "Boyle's Law". Less well known is the fact that he wrote a book entitled *The Wisdom of God Manifested in the Works of Creation*. Newton has been called "the greatest scientist of all time". In addition to giving us his famous laws of motion, he contributed brilliantly to the fields of optics, astronomy, and that branch of mathematics called differential calculus. Yet Newton wrote theological as well as scientific books, and regarded his theological works as more important.

From a later period we may single out Michael Faraday (1791–1867) who discovered electromagnetism, and Sir James Young Simpson (1811–70), the first surgeon to use the anaesthetic properties of chloroform. In this way he paved the way for safe, painless surgery. So did Lord Joseph Lister (1827–1912) who pioneered antiseptic surgery, and saved thousands of lives and a great deal of suffering.

Each of these brilliant scientists had a deep personal faith. Simpson was asked to name his greatest discovery. He is reported to have replied, "It is not chloroform. My greatest discovery has been to know that I am a sinner and that I could be saved by the grace of God."

Louis Pasteur (1822–95), the French chemist who gave his name to pasteurised milk, is another distinguished example. So is Gregor Mendel (1822–84), whose researches into the laws of heredity form the basis of the modern science of genetics. Mendel was an Austrian monk, who became abbot of his monastery.

In seventeenth-century England the Royal Society – a gathering of leading scientists – dedicated its work "to the Glory of God the Creator, and the benefit of the human race". Two centuries later the British Association for the Advancement of Science held its first meeting in York. Those who gathered at that meeting in 1831 paid tribute to the Church, "without whose aid the Association would never have been founded". They went on to declare that "true religion and true science ever lead to the same great end". The Association's first two presidents were clergymen.

. . . and now: The scientist and Christian combination continues today. John Habgood – now Archbishop of York – was a research scientist. Several more professional scientists are convinced Christians, many of whom have written about the relationships between science and Christianity: Ted Evans, Professor of Auditory Physiology, and Donald Mackay, Emeritus Professor of Communication (he is an expert on communication theory and the brain), both of Keele University; Frank Rhodes, one-time Professor of Geology at Michigan University, now President of Cornell; Malcolm Jeeves, Professor of Psychology at St. Andrew's University; Douglas Spanner, Professor Emeritus in Plant Biophysics at London University; Sir John Houghton, Head of the Meteorological Office in London, Fellow of the Royal Society, and previously an Oxford professor; Walter Thorson, Professor of Theoretical Physics at Alberta University in Canada; and George Kinoti, Professor of Zoology at Nairobi University, are distinguished examples from a much longer list. The Research Scientists Christian Fellowship in Britain has some 700 members. Its American counterpart has a membership of about 2,000.

So what? What is the significance of all this? It is not accidental that so many early scientists were men of strong Christian faith, and I will expand on this in Chapter 7. But at this stage I want to make clear what I am *not* saying.

By giving this impressive list of names, I am not trying to prove that Christianity is true. If every scientist in the world was a practising Christian it would not prove this. The evidence for Christianity is to be found mainly in the areas of *history* and *personal experience*, not in science – although the evidence is none the less impressive for that.

Not that all scientists are followers of Christ, of course; far from it. Convinced Christians are in a minority in every job (except ministers of churches, of course!). We would not expect to find a majority of scientists – nor bus drivers, dustmen or teachers – to be believers. And it is well known that some scientists have recorded their *dis*-belief in Christianity.

The list of distinguished names does not prove that Christianity is true. What it *does* show is that Christianity and science are not opposed. The sixth-former was wrong. *For if two teams really are competing against each other, no key player can be on both sides at the same time*. And because most scientists are intelligent people, the fact that a fair number of scientists are Christians also suggests that Christianity is not just a fairy story, suitable only for those who cannot think for themselves.

If it is true that Christianity and science are not opposed, why do so many people think that they are? The seeds of this distortion were sown in two famous conflicts, and we shall consider these. But there are other factors, too. For one thing, unlike so many of the *founders* of modern science, several later *popularisers* of science were militant atheists. They spread their beliefs with missionary zeal.

Their atheism did not arise directly from scientific investigation, although they sometimes gave this impression. By the time they spread their views, scientific method was firmly established. Science was able to cut free from its Christian origins, and develop a life of its own. God appeared to be redundant.

This view has been reinforced by some modern scientists who vigorously express their conviction that God does not exist. They believe that the universe is without ultimate meaning or purpose. Some assert that the "chance" factor which operates in sub-atomic physics lends support to their beliefs.

These views are strongly opposed by scientists who are Christians. To them, the vastness of space, the complexity of matter, and the elegant simplicity of the basic mathematics "behind" it all, point to the marvellous mind of the Maker. But the "science versus religion" controversy is seen at its sharpest in two famous incidents. Two names sum it up: Galileo and Darwin.

Galileo and the heresy trial

The brilliant Italian astronomer Galileo Galilei (1564–1642) was persecuted by the Church of his day for arguing that the earth is not the centre of the universe. It was not a question of an atheist fighting against the Christians. Galileo was a devout Catholic who believed in God just as much as the church leaders. It was a clash between two views about authority, and the correct approach to truth.

Of course, this doesn't excuse the Church leaders for their blind attitude and appalling actions. But it is worth noting that many of Galileo's closest friends and strongest supporters were clergy. Also significant is the fact that Galileo was building on the work of Nicolaus Copernicus (1473–1543). Copernicus laid the foundation for the scientific revolution by suggesting – on mathematical grounds – that the earth travels round the sun. He held office in the Polish Church as a canon of Frauenburg Cathedral. Copernicus described God as "the Best and Most Orderly Workman of all".

Charles Darwin and evolution

In 1859 Charles Darwin published his book *The Origin of Species by Means of Natural Selection*. He put forward the view that life on earth has evolved into higher and higher forms over a long period. But the early chapters of Genesis give a different explanation. We read there that God created the world in six days. It seemed that if Darwin was right, the Bible must be wrong. There was an almighty rumpus.

As with the Galileo controversy, it is significant to notice how the opponents lined up. Some scientists (e.g., Richard

Owen, a leading biologist) ridiculed Darwin's theory. In contrast, some Christians (e.g., the clergyman Charles Kingsley, and F. J. A. Hort, a distinguished Cambridge theologian) welcomed Darwin's researches in the name of truth. But some other churchmen, notably Bishop Samuel Wilberforce, attacked Darwin. A lasting – and false – impression was given. Popular history records the event as "the Church *versus* Evolution". Game, set and match to evolution.

It is most interesting to notice where Charles Darwin himself stood. Because of the controversy caused by his *Origin of Species* and *Descent of Man*, he is often thought to be a great enemy of the Christian Faith. It is true that he wrote, "I gradually came to disbelieve in Christianity as a divine revelation". But he did not intend to undermine Christianity. He spoke about "The Creator" and used a quotation which spoke of the need to study "God's word" and "God's works".

Lord Tennyson, the poet, asked Darwin whether his theory of evolution attacked Christianity, and Darwin replied, "No, certainly not."

This statement is reinforced by Darwin's attitude to missionary work. Early in his career he travelled widely on HMS *Beagle*, gathering material for scientific research. During the five-year voyage his ship visited Tierra del Fuego, at the southern tip of South America. Darwin knew, from personal observation, that the inhabitants of that island were very primitive. When he heard that Christian missionaries were going there, he thought that they were bound to fail. He was wrong, and he was humble enough to admit it. In 1870 he wrote to the South American Missionary Society – an Anglican society which continues to do great work today:

The success of the Tierra del Fuego Mission is most wonderful, and charms me, as I always prophesied utter failure. It is a grand success. I shall feel proud if your committee think fit to elect me an honorary member of your society.

And so we find Charles Darwin, eleven years after the publication of his most controversial book, in the unexpected role of supporter of Christian missionary work. He was compelled to that position by the sheer weight of the evidence: the evidence of the power of Christianity in action.

What then of Genesis?

"In the beginning God created the heavens and the earth . . ." These opening verses of the Bible were read to the world by the Apollo 8 team as they circled the moon on Christmas Day 1968. If it is true that the argument between science and Christianity has lost its heat, how has it been resolved? In particular, what are we to make of those chapters in Genesis which describe the creation of the world. It was these passages which were at the centre of the controversy.

This is one of those areas where we find a variety of opinions among Christians. This was demonstrated very clearly in 1985 by the publication of a book designed as a forum for debate on this question. The book, entitled *Creation and Evolution* (Editor: Derek Burke), has eight contributors, most of whom are distinguished scientists. They were carefully chosen to ensure that a wide range of opinions emerged. Some of them contest views held by most scientists, for example about the age of our earth. Their discussion is too complex to summarise, but I set out below three viewpoints which are most commonly expressed on this issue today.

1. Some maintain that the early chapters in Genesis should be taken literally. As far as they are concerned, the battle is still on. If the theory of evolution appears to clash with the Bible, so much the worse for the theory of evolu-

tion. They point out that some philosophers (e.g. Karl Popper) criticise the theory as not being truly scientific, and that Darwin's views have been considerably modified by later scientists.

Verna Wright is Professor of Rheumatology at Leeds University. In *Creation and Evolution* he writes:

> For myself I believe in a six-day creation. A straight-forward reading of Genesis by an intelligent man, not exposed to the evolutionary model, would suggest a literal six-day creation. The only way around this inter-pretation would be to suggest the account was allegorical or poetic. Neither in the opening chapters of Genesis nor elsewhere in the Bible is there a suggestion that the account is symbolic. Moreover, it is not found in the poetic section of the Old Testament.

He goes on to remind us that the Ten Commandments contain the phrase "for in six days the Lord made heaven and earth". He adds: "With respect, it is worth reminding ourselves that it was the Creator himself who was speak-ing." Views held by a professional scientist, on a subject which he has studied closely, must be weighed carefully.

2. Many Christians strongly disagree with this approach. Some believe that this insistence on "Special Creation" hampers evangelism – drawing the attention of non-believers away from Jesus and onto sterile secondary issues. They are worried that unbelievers will write off the Church as "anti-science", and shut their ears to the claims of Christ.

They point out that astronomers speak of the vast age of the universe (the "big bang" took place some 15,000 million years ago, and events of momentous significance occurred in the first three minutes, according to current theory). They note, too, that despite modifications to

Darwin's theory, the majority of biologists think that there are good grounds for accepting evolution.

As a result they maintain that it is quite possible to accept the theory of evolution *and* the Bible. The Bible tells us *that* God created the world and all living creatures; scientific theories like evolution attempt to tell us *how* he did it. They may go on to point out that the order of creation in Genesis 1 is similar to that suggested by scientists investigating the origins of life on earth (e.g., water creatures before animals). They may suggest that the six "days" of creation in Genesis represent very long periods of time.

3. Other Christians agree broadly with this view, but argue that even the points about order and time are not really important. They maintain that it is essential to view the early chapters of Genesis as *pre*-scientific or *non*-scientific literature. They were written centuries before the rise of modern science. Whether or not they square with the findings of scientists is therefore unimportant, for the author – or editor(s) – was not concerned with modern scientific questions.

The description of the Creation in Genesis, and theories developed within modern science, do not *agree* or *disagree* with each other, because they use different types of language and are concerned with different problems. Dr. Alan Richardson expressed this viewpoint when he said that Genesis "is dealing with matters beyond the scope of science".

Central to these last two views is the idea that *literal* truth is not the only *real* truth. We are, of course, quite used to accepting statements as true, even though we would not dream of taking them literally.

I lost my head	She's an old battle-axe
I smell a rat	He's got a frog in his throat
Get your act together	I jumped out of my skin

When Robert Burns wrote "O my Luve's like a red, red rose" we understand that he did not mean that every embrace was extremely painful. Nor that his girlfriend's complexion suggested that she was prone to nosebleeds!

The Bible often uses vivid picture language of this kind. I doubt that the Psalmist really saw the hills clapping their hands, or skipping like lambs. And St. Peter reminds us that in God's eyes, one day and one thousand years amount to the same thing (2 Pet. 3:8).

The same kind of principle applies to the parables of Jesus. Did the Prodigal Son or the Good Samaritan exist outside the imagination of Jesus? Did he really know of a widow who pestered a judge, or a woman who lost a coin? Perhaps; perhaps not. It simply does not matter. We would not accuse Jesus of lying if he invented those characters to illustrate the truths he wanted to communicate. To do so would be like refusing to take a novel seriously because the characters are fictitious! Parables and novels can teach profound truths without being *literally* true.

The same approach can be applied to the early chapters of Genesis. We can believe that the accounts of the Creation were inspired by God, without maintaining that Genesis is intended to give a literal, scientifically exact, account of the way in which the world began. We must not judge it as though this was the intention.

But it is true. It teaches vitally important truths about God, about us, and about the world in which we live.

God created the world. Human beings are the "crown" of God's creation. We were given freedom and responsibility. The first human beings rebelled against God, and this rebellion affected the subsequent history of the world. All these truths are found in those first few chapters of the Bible. They are expressed there with a superb, poetic artistry which can be understood by people of all ages and cultures.

But Genesis doesn't only give us a history lesson. With

clear insight it focusses our own personal conflicts. We see mirrored in Adam and Eve our own personal fall from innocence; our own struggles with temptation; our own fears; our own corruption; our own self-deception; our own desire to wriggle out of responsibility for our actions. (Adam said it was Eve's fault; Eve quickly passed the parcel to the serpent. Only yesterday I caught myself at the same game!)

On the basis of reading the first few chapters of Genesis and taking them seriously but not literally, what sort of world would we expect to find? We should expect a world in which there is a great deal of beauty and design, *plus* a great deal of trouble and disharmony. In short, we would expect to find the world *as it actually is*.

This is the genius of the book of Genesis. It describes and explains the human situation in a most profound way. The glory and the tragedy are both there. Genesis raises deep questions about our relationship with God, with nature, and with other people. The rest of the Bible shows the solution to these vital questions being worked out in the lives of individuals and nations.

Such literature is every bit as important as a scientific treatise on the origins of the universe.

6

MORE ABOUT CHRISTIANITY AND SCIENCE

There are basically three ways of viewing the relationship between science and Christianity. The "antagonistic view" suggests that science has disproved religion, and we examined that in the previous chapter. In this chapter we consider two other views.

1. God is in there somewhere
Some Christians, knowing that scientists are explaining more and more, look anxiously for gaps in scientific knowledge. They assert that God is at work in these gaps in a way

which is beyond scientific explanation. In this way they hope to defend the existence of God in a scientific age. We cannot do without God, they maintain, for the gaps in scientific knowledge can only be accounted for by his direct activity. For obvious reasons, this view is sometimes called "the God of the gaps".

It is a fatal approach for two reasons:

a) The gaps in scientific knowledge are still enormous, but they are shrinking all the time. What was a large gap ten years ago may be a very small gap, or no gap at all, now. Hence God appears to be squeezed out.

b) This view is based on a false understanding of the relationship between God and his Creation. The Bible teaches that God is "behind" or "upholds" the *whole* of Creation, not just the puzzling parts. He is every bit as responsible for those areas which *can* be explained by scientists, as those which (as yet, anyway) *cannot*.

This defensive view, or God of the gaps, is as false as the antagonistic view.

2. Two ways of looking at the same thing
This is by far the most satisfactory approach to the problem. Christianity and science view and explain things from two *different*, but *equally valid*, angles.

One common way of expressing this is to say that science asks *how?* questions (*how* does this work?), while religion asks *why?* questions. This oversimplifies the position but it remains a useful distinction. (The fact that deep *why?* questions are asked by ordinary people was brought home to me by a young child. She turned thoughtfully from looking out of a window and asked: "Why is there anything at all?" Those in the know will recall that the philosopher Martin Heidegger posed the same question: "Why is there something, and not nothing?")

A few everyday examples will illustrate the principle behind this approach.

People: A newspaper article suggested that Miss World is in reality a collection of chemicals, costing a few pounds. We see from this the importance of taking more than one viewpoint into account. And it shows the danger of phrases like "nothing but", "only", "merely" and "nothing more than".

Miss World, like the rest of us, *is* made up of chemicals. But she is not *only* or *nothing but* a mixture of chemicals. Ask the television audience! It is perfectly valid to view human beings from the point of view of their chemical composition. It is *not* valid to suggest that this is the only viewpoint which matters.

Similarly, it can be useful – and accurate – to think of a person as a machine, or as an advanced animal, or as a walking computer. The fatal mistake is to think that by describing him in these ways, we rule out other viewpoints – a spiritual viewpoint for example. To say that man is an animal (a "naked ape") is one thing. To say that man is *only* an animal is something quite different.

Objects: Any object can be viewed from a variety of viewpoints which complement, or add to, one another. For example, a diamond may be regarded by a millionaire as an article giving prestige, by a geologist as a piece of native crystallised carbon with a hardness of 10, and by an engaged couple as a symbol of their love. To ask which single viewpoint is the right one shows a lack of understanding. *Each* of them is correct.

Events: Events can be explained from different viewpoints as well. They can be described in *scientific* terms and in *personal* terms.

A window is broken. Why?

Answer in scientific terms: When a missile weighing four ounces, and travelling at 60 miles per hour, strikes a pane of glass 2mm thick, the glass will shatter.

Answer in personal terms: Johnny Green has made a catapult. Johnny Green is crying. Why?

Answer in scientific terms: When a missile the weight of a man's hand, and travelling at 40 miles per hour, strikes the skin, the nerve ends are aggravated.

Answer in personal terms: Johnny Green's dad was so wild when he received the bill for a new window that he slapped his son's rump with considerable vigour.

To ask which of these explanations is correct is clearly absurd. It is not a question of either/or. We have two completely different explanations and *both are correct*.

Of course, one of the explanations may be more *appropriate* to the situation than the other. If you had given Johnny's dad the scientific explanation to his angry question about the broken window, he would have been even more angry! But both explanations are true, even though only one is sufficiently relevant to be worth stating.

This principle applies to everything. Why is the kettle boiling? When the temperature of water is raised to 100° Celsius (at standard pressure), rapid evaporation takes place. Why is the kettle boiling? It is 4 o'clock, and old Mrs. Brown always makes a cup of tea at that time. And so we could go on. But we must return to the central question. What has this to do with science and religion?

God and Nature: What applies to everyday events – the broken window, the boiling kettle – can be applied to really big events as well.

Why does the earth support life? It is quite possible to give an answer in scientific terms. Factors like the importance of carbon, and the size of the earth being just right to support an atmosphere, will be mentioned. But it is equally possible to give an explanation in "personal" terms – by maintaining that God designed the earth so that these factors apply. If this is the case, then scientists are discovering the way in which God has designed the world. By doing so they help us to see his greatness.

Hence Sir James Jeans could speak of God as a mathematician, and Kepler, the brilliant early astronomer, could say that he was "thinking God's thoughts after Him". Dr. Malcolm Dixon, a biochemist, put it clearly. "If we believe that God made the world, have we the slightest ground for saying that He did not do it through the operation of natural laws and natural forces? . . . Surely not."

It is, of course, open to anyone to disagree with the explanation in terms of the activity of God. Others may wish to explain it as the result of chance, not as the work of God. But it is *not* open to anyone to disagree with the explanation in terms of God just *because* science can explain how the earth supports life.

The fact that science can give an explanation does not, and cannot, disprove the explanation in personal terms. To suggest this is like arguing that the scientific explanation for Johnny Green's stinging bottom proves that his father did not hit him! The two explanations are complementary. They can stand side by side.

To sum up: scientists – *as* scientists – cannot comment on whether God is "behind" the universe or not, because this is not a scientific question. As thoughtful human beings they will, of course, have views on this matter. Science does not and cannot disprove religion. Nor does it prove religion to be true. Science and religion look at the universe from different viewpoints, and ask different sets of important questions.

CONCLUDING QUOTATION

"It is the contention of the Christian that, in order to do full justice to the totality of his experience, he finds it necessary to see and interpret the over-all pattern of his experience not only in biochemical, physiological or psychological terms, but also in religious terms." – *Malcolm Jeeves, Professor of Psychology at St Andrew's University.*

TAKE A BREAK (3)

Confessions by the author (all true, I promise!)
As a young curate, my ministry got off to a rather bad start. My local paper reported that I would be working at St. Dude's. An excusable mistake no doubt; St. Jude isn't the best known of saints, and I confess that I did feel rather like a Dude, in my brand-new dog collar.

* * *

Then there was the youth club. I sauntered in – rather like a Dude, I suppose – and casually picked up a table-tennis bat. Soon I was playing a hard match, and trying desperately to impress.

At the first opportunity I made an exotic smash. Then the trouble began. My fast-moving arm hit a bystander who was drinking a bottle of coke. Result: one youth club member was minus one tooth.

He was very understanding and he freely forgave me. Fortunately, one of the church lay-readers was an excellent dentist. Some years later, when I was working at a college in Sussex, a new student introduced herself. "Bob Mills is our church youth club leader," she said. "He sends greetings, and he still forgives you for knocking out his tooth!"

* * *

The table-tennis incident was followed by further embarrassment. We were voting for PCC members. Whether or not curates should vote, I don't know, but I did. On my ballot paper I listed all the names, then crossed them out as I put them in rank order. Result: one very scruffy voting paper.

When the ballot was over a small group of us were asked to go to another room to count the votes. As we counted, one of my colleagues stopped with a snort. "Really," she exclaimed, "some of our people are almost illiterate." To prove her point she passed round my voting paper. To my shame, I looked at it, agreed with her, and passed it on.

7

COMMON GROUND

We have noted some of the differences between science and religion, but it is important to observe that they share some common ground. I will mark out four areas.

1. How science began
At this point, I invite you to take part in the world's shortest questionnaire. Please tick a, b or c.

a) Without Jesus there would be no modern science.

b) Nonsense: Jesus had nothing to do with the rise of science.

c) The answer lies somewhere between a) and b).

No Jesus; no science! This provocative statement *could*

be right. We can't prove it, of course – because we cannot imagine what the world would be like without his immense influence. But the actual truth is almost as startling. *Christian faith gave birth to modern science.*

This isn't my own cranky personal view. For example, the historian Herbert Butterfield affirmed that science is a child of Christian thought. The philosophers A. N. Whitehead and John MacMurray made the same point. MacMurray affirmed that "Science is the legitimate child of a great religious movement, and its genealogy goes back to Jesus."

Those who take this view emphasise that science could only get under way when certain factors were present. One of the most important ingredients was the correct mental approach. For true science to develop it was vital that certain beliefs about the nature of the world should be widespread. The belief that:

– matter is essentially good
– the same laws apply everywhere
– human beings are called to be stewards of creation
– time moves forward in a straight line, rather than round in circles

These views are expounded in the Bible. In contrast, some religions teach that matter is evil, or that we should be detached from the world, or that different gods rule different aspects of life, or that time goes round in endless cycles.

Some ancient Greeks and medieval Arabs were very good at mathematics, and deeply interested in scientific questions. There were important advances. But in the event, it was Christian civilisation which brought science to birth. Dr. Peter Hodgson, Lecturer in Nuclear Physics at Oxford University, puts it this way: "Christianity provided just those beliefs that are essential for science, and the whole moral climate that encouraged its growth."

2. Science and religion need each other

Science – and its offspring, technology – have transformed our world. The spectacular success of science over the last three hundred years has given it massive authority. Religion, too, continues to make a considerable impact on individuals and societies – sometimes, alas, for ill rather than for good. But at their best, the world's many religions spread love, justice and understanding.

Science and religion need each other. To give one example: the energetic drive to arrest leprosy has been spearheaded by Christians. This campaign of compassion is based on obedience to the call of Jesus (Matt. 10:8) *and* on the techniques of modern medical skill.

But scientific discoveries can be used for good or ill. The dark shadows cast by germ and nuclear warfare are chilling reminders of this. And in medicine, impressive new techniques present complex ethical questions. Our troubled and divided world needs wisdom, compassion and sensitivity, as never before.

Christians don't claim a monopoly on these qualities. But if the Christian Faith is true, they should be in evidence in the community of believers – and readily available for use in our world of dangerous tension and difficult decision-making.

3. Science and religion both put limits on "commonsense"

As a Londoner living in Yorkshire I have come to value commonsense. There's a lot of it about in these parts! We are right to place a high value upon it, for it is another word for practical wisdom, or good decision-making.

But science sounds a warning bell about commonsense. Recently I stood on a cliff-top. It jutted out, and as I looked at the sea on three sides, two things were quite clear. Firstly, the earth is flat. Secondly, if I ventured near the edge of that saucer-shaped horizon, I should fall off. That was the verdict of commonsense.

The verdict of science – that I was standing on a sphere

from which I could not fall, even if I wanted to – seemed very far-fetched. But I accept that verdict, not the verdict of my eyes.

Shortly after that day out, I heard a radio programme on science and religion. The scientists agreed that they often have to ignore or press beyond, the commonsense "obvious" explanation. A stone might appear to be solid. Look "closer" and you are dealing with empty space, and packets of energy.

One of those scientists was a Christian, and he discussed the question of paradox. He noted that for decades scientists had to live with two irreconcilable views of the nature of light. One set of data told them that light is made up of a stream of particles. Other evidence told them that light is a series of waves. About one thing they were clear: it couldn't be both! But in 1928 a scientist solved this puzzle. Paul Dirac invented quantum field theory, which is able to integrate all the information.

On the radio, that scientist went on to say that Christianity sometimes challenges commonsense in the same kind of way. How can God be three in one? How could Jesus be both God and man? In his view, such puzzles have the ring of reality about them. He certainly didn't want to hide behind mysteries. But as a scientist he is used to finding surprises when he is dealing with deep questions at the limits of our understanding.

Christianity does not require us to believe a hundred impossible things before breakfast. But – like science – it sometimes asks us to be adventurous enough to cope with such surprises, and to question "obvious" everyday beliefs.

4. Science and Christianity both acknowledge limitations

The whole purpose of scientific activity is to press back the frontiers of knowledge; to replace ignorance by understanding. Most religions are involved in a similar quest – though the questions they put are different from scientific questions. Why are we here? What happens when we die? Is there purpose in life? Does God exist? How can we cope with evil within our own hearts and lives? These are questions with which the Christian Faith grapples – questions which ultimately face us all.

Science and Christianity both ask questions in an attitude of humility. At least, their best practitioners do. St. Paul summed up the Christian position like this: "Now we see but a poor reflection; then we shall see face to face. Now I know in part; then I shall know fully, even as I am fully known" (1 Cor. 13:12). Ancient mirrors gave an imperfect reflection; total clarity was rare. This is St. Paul's point.

We *do* have light by which to live. Christians believe that this light shines at its brightest in the person of Jesus. But there are many answers about the riddle of life at which we can only guess.

God deals with us in a very practical manner. Our curiosity is great, and we should like light on a whole range of questions. Instead, God gives us just enough to be getting on with. We are like people with a powerful torch on a dark night. The torch lights up the path, but it doesn't enable us to see the surrounding countryside. One day, however, we shall see the whole majestic view, in the light of eternity.

In the same way, modern scientists know that their understanding is limited. In earlier centuries, some scientists believed that nature would inevitably yield all her secrets to their investigations. In these days of quarks, gluons and black holes in space, they acknowledge "that nature is now seen to be mysterious; much of it is unknown, unknowable and unfathomable." Those words were written by Professor Harold Schilling, a distinguished American physicist. Dr. Lewis Thomas, another scientist, makes the same point: "We do not understand much of anything . . . we have a wilderness of mystery to make our way through in the centuries ahead."

CONCLUDING QUOTATIONS

Science without religion is lame, religion without science is blind – *Albert Einstein, who revolutionised modern physics with his Theory of Relativity*.

During the past thirty years people from all the civilised countries of the earth have consulted me . . . Among my patients in the second half of life – that is to say over thirty-five – there has not been one whose problem in the last resort was not that of finding a religious outlook on life – *Carl Gustav Jung, one of the great founders of modern psychology*.

Religion and natural science are fighting a joint battle in an incessant, never relaxing crusade against scepticism and against dogmatism, against disbelief and against super-stition, and the rallying cry in this crusade has always been, and always will be: "On to God" – *Max Planck, awarded the Nobel Prize for his work on the Quantum Theory*.

Science brings man nearer to God – *Louis Pasteur, who revolutionised microbiology*.

Historically, religion came first and science grew out of religion. Science has never superseded religion, and it is my expectation that it never will supersede it – *the eminent historian Arnold Toynbee*.

*   *   *

Note: the four areas discussed in this chapter by no means cover all the common ground between science and religion. For example, recent authors have drawn attention to the importance of faith and intuition in science; to the fact that modern scientific activity is often corporate (indeed, inter-national) in nature; and to the sense of awe and wonder sometimes evoked by scientific investigation.

8

A SHORT CHAPTER ABOUT A LONG CLIMB

In 1961 Yuri Gagarin became the first human being in space. On his return to earth, it was widely reported that he had not seen God "up there". This naive assertion still rumbles, and it deserves a naive reply. No doubt Yuri G. spoke with tongue in cheek – which is how I am writing.

When I broadcast the following "parable" on local radio, it seemed to catch the imagination. Margaret Howard selected it for her *Pick of the Week* on Radio 4, and I received many letters and phone calls requesting a copy. In view of this, I decided to include this little tale as a "fun" postscript to the hard work of the previous three chapters. When broadcast it was adorned by Scott Joplin's "The Entertainer". Alas, modern technology is as yet unable to reproduce this music from the printed page.

Perhaps I should add that the original, excellent, idea wasn't mine. Sadly, I don't know whose idea it was; it came to my notice as an aside in a long-forgotten conversation. But the parable itself is my handiwork; I alone am to blame!

*   *   *

Once upon a time there lived a community of mice. They lived in a large house, and their front door was a hole in the skirting board of the music room. In the music room there was a grand piano, and from time to time they heard beautiful music.

"Ah," they would say. "Beautiful," they would sigh. But sometimes the music stirred debate. Deep debate. There was a piano – of that they were sure. And there was beautiful music – of that they were sure, too. But . . . was there a musician?

Some were quite certain. "Stuff and nonsense" said the atheists. "If we could see inside the piano we should understand how music is made. All this talk of design and intention is quite unnecessary."

"Stuff and nonsense," said the believing mice. "You are quite wrong. Beautiful music like that certainly doesn't happen by chance. If there is music, there must be a musician." "Stuff and nonsense," said the agnostic mice. "We simply don't have enough evidence to decide one way or the other. We are in the dark and we shall remain in the dark. Get on with sharing the cheese."

Within the community there was one especially curious mouse called – yes, you've guessed it – Michael. One day he decided to go on an adventure of discovery. He would settle this question; and he would settle it *now*.

He crept to the hole in the skirting board, and began to climb the leg of the grand piano. When he was halfway up, the beautiful music started again. With the greatest difficulty he climbed the shiny sheer surface. He was bursting with curiosity. Just what would he see?

At last he completed his climb and peered inside. He looked, he gasped, and he scampered down the leg, across the floor and back through the hole in the wall. As he returned the entire community gathered around. "What did you see?" they demanded, in great excitement.

"I climbed the leg of the piano," panted Michael, "and I looked inside the piano . . . and I saw how music is made!"

There was a deep silence. Michael caught his breath and he continued, "I saw lots of little wooden hammers striking against lots of metal wires . . . *I saw . . . no pianist.*"

That night, as they went to bed, some were jubilant. They had been proved right. The pianist was a myth; a figment of the imagination. Others had mixed feelings. It was good to know the truth, but they were disappointed just the same. Others were downright sad. It wasn't simply that they had been proved wrong. It was bigger than that. Life was rather less interesting than they had hoped, and rather more empty. It seemed that, after all, there really was nothing more to do than to get on with sharing and eating the cheese.

Part III

Questions about the Bible

The existence of the Bible is the greatest blessing which humanity ever experienced.

Immanuel Kant

A multi-million-pound con-job.

Anonymous

Men turn this way and that in their search for new sources of comfort and inspiration, but the enduring truths are to be found in the word of God.

Queen Elizabeth the Queen Mother

9

YOU CAN'T BELIEVE THE BIBLE TODAY

A friend of mine conducted some street interviews for local radio. On one occasion his subject was the Bible. One person dismissed it as "a multi-million-pound con-job". This extreme response wasn't common, but it became clear that many people feel very unsure about the reliability of the Bible.

A best-seller? Certainly. Interesting? Possibly. But when

it comes to the really important question of *truth* – more fiction than fact.

If they are right, this is extremely damaging to the Christian Faith, for we are largely dependent upon the New Testament for our information about Jesus. This is the only place where we find anything like a full account of his ministry.

Certainly, it is a less detailed account than we might wish. But – the crucial question – is it an *accurate* account? Christianity demands that we should drastically alter our lives. In return, we are right to demand that it should produce strong credentials.

A: BASED ON ACCURATE RECORDS?

The procedure for assessing the reliability of the New Testament is the same as for any other important ancient document, when the original no longer exists. There are two vital factors, both of which depend on the discovery of copies of the original.

The first factor involves the *number* of copies which have been found. The second concerns the *age* of these copies – the time lag between the original document and the copies which now exist.

We can be confident that we possess an accurate record when (1) we find several copies which are basically similar, and (2) the copies we have are fairly near in time to the original author.

A time span which seems great to us will satisfy the experts, provided there are enough copies to enable them to cross-check. (Provided, also, that these copies were not all taken from the same earlier copy.) Here is a table which compares the four Gospels with some other famous ancient manuscripts.

Ancient Writing	Thucy-dides' HISTORY	Caesar's GALLIC WAR	Tacitus' HISTORIES	The Four Gos-pels
(A) Date of original document	460–400 BC	58–50 BC	AD 100	AD 65–90
(B) Oldest surviving copy	AD 900 (plus a few 1st century fragments)	AD 850	AD 800	*
(C) Approx. time between A and B	1300 years (fragments 400 years)	900 years	700 years	*
(D) Number of ancient copies in existence today	8	10	2	*

In order to get the strength of the evidence for the Gospels, I invite you to put your own estimates in the spaces marked with an asterisk in the diagram. We shall consider the bottom line (D) first.

1. How many?

It proved difficult to find an accurate figure for the number of existing ancient hand-written copies of the Gospels in Greek – the language in which they were originally written. To solve the problem I wrote to Tyndale House in

Cambridge – a centre which specialises in Biblical research.

They could not give me an accurate figure either, for the list is too long to count without taking a very long time! For copies made before AD 1000 they suggested that I should use the ·phrase "many hundreds, hundreds upon hundreds". Compare this with 8, 10 and 2, and you can see that the Gospels are in a different league altogether.

2. How long?

Now to the time factor. There are two existing copies of the New Testament dated AD 350 – less than three hundred years after the original. This compares very favourably with the 1300, 900, and 700 years for the other books listed in the chart (see row C). One of these very old copies of the New Testament is in the Vatican Library. The other is in the British Museum. The British Government bought it from the Soviet Government on Christmas Day 1933, for £100,000 – a tremendous bargain! (The USSR continues to hold – in Leningrad – the oldest surviving complete copy of the Hebrew Scriptures, apart from the Dead Sea Scrolls.)

When we take into account incomplete copies of the New Testament, the situation is even more impressive – a few excellent manuscripts are 100 to 200 years earlier still. Some of the Chester Beatty and Bodmer Papyri are dated before AD 250. Each of these contains copies of the Gospels. The Bodmer copy of St. John was made as early as AD 200 and contains about two-thirds of the complete Gospel. The earliest discovery of all is a fragment from John's Gospel. It is dated at a breathtaking AD 130 (see page 111).

Parts are found because portions of some manuscripts are destroyed or lost, and also because scribes sometimes· copied only one section of the New Testament. Start copying all twenty-seven books and you will see why!

Summary

As with the number, so with the time gap: the evidence for the Gospels is streets ahead of other ancient documents. No one doubts that we have a reliable text of Caesar's Gallic War and the rest. The case for the reliability of the New Testament is far stronger.

I will call on Bishop John Robinson to sum up. He is a particularly interesting witness because of his radical credentials. His book *Honest to God* sold millions of copies around the world, and showed that he was not afraid to rock the boat.

His much better book *Can We Trust the New Testament?* has sold far fewer copies, probably because of its much more orthodox conclusions. But his conclusions do not arise from a loss of nerve. Up to his untimely death in 1984, he continued to follow the argument wherever the evidence led him. This is what he said on the subject under discussion:

> To return to the textual transmission of the New Testament, the wealth of manuscripts, and above all the narrow interval of time between the writing and the earliest extant copies, make it by far the best-attested text of any ancient writing in the world.

He also draws on the Oxford classical historian, A. N. Sherwin-White, who "chides New Testament scholars for failing to recognise what by any comparable standards excellent sources they have!"

This view is shared by other scholars: "There is much more evidence for the New Testament than for other ancient writings of comparable date" (F. F. Bruce). "In spite of the numerous possibilities for error, the New Testament is probably the most trustworthy piece of writing that has survived from antiquity" (M. C. Tenney). "The New Testament manuscripts in our possession are much closer in time to the original writings, more numerous and in closer agreement with each other than any other ancient book" (Hans Küng).

B: BASED ON ACCURATE MEMORIES?

We can be confident, then, about modern translations of the New Testament. They are based on ancient documents which faithfully record what St. Mark and the others wrote. But can we also be sure that the Gospel writers accurately recorded the life and death of Jesus in the first place?

This apparently straightforward question leads us into a minefield of dispute! According to some theologians the question itself is misleading. They assert that the four Gospels are concerned with theology, not history. On this view Matthew, Mark, Luke and John were much more interested in the question, *"What is the significance of Jesus?"* than with the question *"What did Jesus do and say?"*

Other theologians disagree. They believe that the Evangelists were interested in *both* these questions, for an event and its significance – history and theology – belong together. No event, no significance! But it has sometimes been left to experts in ancient history and literature, not theology, to insist on the overall historical reliability of the Gospels.

Having weighed the various issues, I continue to be convinced that four questions take us to the heart of the matter.

1. *Could* they have invented the material?
Jesus lived in the public eye from about AD 27 to AD 30, when he was crucified. The Gospels are very largely concerned with those three years.

Mark's Gospel was probably the first to be completed – by about AD 65. It is likely that large parts of Matthew and

Luke – especially those parts which record the teaching of Jesus – were written down by AD 50, some twenty years after his death.

This seems a long time until we remember that the early Christians were much less concerned than we are with writing, and much more concerned with speaking and memorising. Even today, some Muslims memorise the entire Qur'ān – their Holy Book. It is shorter than the Bible, but substantial none the less. No wonder Professor Nineham could write about "the wonderfully retentive memory of the Oriental"!

In the days of Jesus, disciples often remembered by rote the teachings of their rabbis. To help them, the rabbis sometimes cast their teachings in poetic form. Jesus certainly did. This can be seen when passages in the Greek New Testament are translated back into Aramaic, the "native" language of Jesus.

Stories were told, and sermons were preached about Jesus from the moment he died. They were written down only when those who had been with him during his life began to run the risk of death, either from persecution or from natural causes. It was rather like a modern lecturer making a book out of the things which he and his colleagues have been saying in their lectures for several years.

A man who was twenty when Jesus was crucified would have been about forty when the teaching material used by Matthew and Luke was written down and circulated – and about fifty-five when Mark completed his account. Indeed, he may have been younger than that. For in *Redating the New Testament* John Robinson argues that the Gospels – and other New Testament books – were written earlier than is commonly supposed.

Thousands heard Jesus teach, and saw him in action. Thousands more heard the preaching about him from the time of his death. If one of the preachers had radically altered the account, there would have been an outcry – from friends and enemies. If the material when written down had been very different from the preaching of the early disciples, a similar protest would have followed.

The fact that there were plenty of eye-witnesses does not guarantee every item in the Gospels, but it does guarantee their *general* reliability. Winston Churchill did great things during the last war, but if someone now suggested that he had healed the sick or fed the crowds, the balloon would soon go up! The span of time since the war is longer than the gap between Jesus and the written record about him.

Another point is raised by the question, "Could the early preachers, or the Gospel writers, have invented the teaching of Jesus?" Quite literally – *could* they? Or are the sayings so majestic that only someone as great as Jesus could have uttered them?

Beverley Nichols made this point very forcibly some years ago.

> You cannot deny the reality of this character, *in whatever body it resided . . . somebody* said, "The Sabbath was made for man, and not man for the Sabbath"; *somebody* said, "For what shall it profit a man if he shall gain the whole world and lose his own soul"; *somebody* said, "Suffer the little children to come unto me, and forbid them not" . . .
>
> *Somebody* said these things, because they are staring me in the face at this moment from the Bible. And whoever said them was *gigantic*. And whoever said them was *living* . . . we cannot find in any contemporary literature any phrases which have a shadow of the beauty, the truth, the individuality, nor the *indestructibility* of those phrases.
>
> And remember, I have only quoted five sentences at random. (From *The Fool Hath Said*)

2. *Would* they have invented the material?

Let's assume for a moment that it was possible for the Gospel writers to invent teaching which they attributed to

Jesus. Or that the preachers and story-tellers from whom they got their material could have got away with distortion. Even if they had the opportunity, would they have done so?

A good deal of the teaching in the Gospels is about morality – including honesty. Is it likely – or even possible – that some of the finest teaching about honesty which the world has ever known is itself part of a huge lie?

Besides which, material which the Church leaders might have been tempted to invent is not included. For example, there was a tremendous argument in the Church, at the time when the Gospel material was being preached and written. Should Gentile Christians be made to keep the Jewish law of circumcision? It nearly split the Church in two.

If Jesus had given clear teaching on this, the matter would have been easily settled. But he didn't; so the Gospels do not contain such teaching. An inventor – even a well-meaning one – would almost certainly have included something on this problem. To quote John Robinson again: "There seems to have been a reverence for the remembered speech and acts of Jesus which provided an inbuilt resistance to the temptation to make him merely their mouthpiece or puppet."

I am not suggesting that human memories of the first century were equivalent to modern tape recorders. Nor that the Gospel writers mechanically recorded all they were told about Jesus. Nothing could be further from the truth.

Each of the Evangelists approached events in the life of Jesus in an individual manner. Slightly different accounts of some of the sayings of Jesus show that, sometimes at least, they summarised his words. Compare, for example, Matthew 26:64 and Mark 14:62.

In my view these differences *add* to the authenticity of the Gospels. It is clear that we are not dealing with a carefully contrived plot. We have honest accounts by honest men. And I repeat my conviction that the end result

is so unexpected and so majestic that invention is out of the
question – a view shared by many others.
(*Note*: If you want to read more about these questions, I
immodestly suggest my modest booklet *God Speaks: the
Bible* (Lion 1986). For a really thorough treatment, read *I
Believe in the Historical Jesus* by I. Howard Marshall
(Hodder 1977)).

3. Do the Gospels ring true today?
The impact of the Gospels on open minds is impressive.
The classical scholar E. V. Rieu was asked by Penguin
Books to make a new translation of the Gospels. On
hearing of the invitation his son is reported to have commented: "It will be very interesting to see what Father
makes of the Gospels; it'll be still more interesting to see
what the Gospels make of Father."

At the end of his lengthy task, Dr. Rieu wrote: "These
documents . . . bear the seal of the Son of Man and God,
they are the Magna Carta of the human spirit."

More recently, an actor made a similar discovery. Alec
McCowen decided to learn St. Mark's Gospel by heart – as
a hobby! He was astonished to find that crowded theatres
around the world wanted to see and hear his solo presenta-
tion of the Gospel. With few props he simply told the
story of Jesus as St. Mark recorded it – a great tribute to
the power of Alec McCowen's acting and of St. Mark's
writing.

The experience made a deep impression on him. He
summed it up like this: "Something absolutely marvellous
happened in Galilee 2,000 years ago."

4. Can we check any of the details?
Yes, we can. In two ways: by internal examination and by
external comparison.

Firstly, we can examine the text itself. When we do this,
we make some remarkable discoveries. Some of these are
small but significant. Don Cupitt suggests that two Aramaic

words (*zakkau* and *dakkau*) point to Luke's integrity as an historian! (in Ian Wilson's *Jesus: the Evidence*). Certainly, two sentences do the same for St. Mark. In one of these Jesus admits his ignorance; in the second he cries out in anguish: *Why?* (see Mark 13:30–32 and 15:34).

Commenting on these passages C. S. Lewis says: "The evangelists have the first great characteristic of honest witnesses: they mention facts which are, at first sight, damaging to their main contention."

Some discoveries are on a larger scale; they can be made only if we study the entire New Testament. For example, Jesus constantly called himself the "Son of Man". In contrast, this title is referred to Jesus in only three other places in the whole New Testament (Acts 7; Rev. 1 and 14). Also significant is the fact that Jesus' emphasis on the Kingdom of God gives way in the preaching of the early Church to three other themes: Jesus himself, and his death and resurrection.

If the New Testament authors invented these and other changes in emphasis and terminology, they were breath-takingly clever. These men were widely dispersed, and without access to telephones or computers. In my view, they would have found it impossible to invent such a subtle story-line, with just the right balance of agreement and divergence. Impossible – unless we add a further invention: a vast flock of well-trained carrier pigeons!

Secondly, we can test the text against a knowledge of history and geography gained from other sources. John Robinson points out that Luke is detailed and accurate at some points, and "extraordinarily vague" at others. He comments: "It is a tribute to him as a historian that where he does not know he does not invent: he generalises." And he cites A. N. Sherwin-White again. This historian studied the trial of Jesus in the light of his detailed knowledge of Roman Law, and of the social practice of the period. He "gave it high marks".

Our ability to check details is often dependent on

archaeological finds. Certainly the science of archaeology continues to throw light upon the whole Bible. But this is an important subject, so we will devote two short chapters to it.

We have been studying historical evidence. Any historical "proof" depends upon two things. Firstly, the facts – the documents, objects, eye-witness accounts, etc. Secondly, the willingness of the investigator to be open to the conclusions to which the facts point.

No one can take you to the Battle of Hastings. If you refuse to believe unless you see it for yourself, then you will never be convinced about anything in history. Not about 1066, nor that Julius Caesar crossed the Rubicon, nor that Jesus taught in Galilee.

Some people refuse to be convinced no matter how strong the evidence. The Flat Earth Society maintained that pictures taken by astronauts were clever fakes. "The earth is flat," they said. End of argument.

The evidence for Christianity is largely concerned with historical proof. All we Christians ask is that the openness of mind which is necessary and proper for the study of history should not be withdrawn just for that period now called the first century AD or CE.

CONCLUDING QUOTATIONS

St. Luke: the most beautiful book ever written – *Ernest Renan*.

Were we to devote to their comprehension (i.e. the Gospels) a little of the selfless enthusiasm that is now expended on the riddle of our physical surroundings, we should cease to say that Christianity is coming to an end – we might even feel that it had only just begun – *E. V. Rieu, on completing his translation of the Gospels*.

Whatever our view of it (St. Mark's Gospel) may be it remains, for good or ill, the most important document in the history of the world, an unrivalled source of information, a corner stone . . .

But the doubter is entitled to ask – "Is it true?" I cannot prove it, I can only testify to it . . . Week after week, year after year I have been sitting down in front of this Gospel seeking to penetrate it, to keep my mind open to it . . . I can only say that this exercise has only served to reinforce a conviction that in this Gospel we are in the presence of historical, elemental truth – *Stuart Blanch, when Archbishop of York, in Living by Faith (D. L. T. 1983)*.

10

WHAT ABOUT THE SOUTH SEA SCROLLS?

The previous chapter mentioned archaeology. The next two chapters will look more closely at the significance of some of the many scrolls, tablets, etc. which have been discovered in recent years.

"The greatest manuscript discovery of modern times"
The question which forms the chapter heading was put to me by a student. He had heard someone claim that some scrolls had disproved the Bible, but he couldn't remember their name!

He was, of course, referring to the Dead Sea Scrolls. They were discovered in 1947 in caves at Qumran on the north-western shore of the Dead Sea. The scrolls had been stored there by a strict community of Jews which flourished during the first centuries BC and AD (from about 150 BC to AD 68).

These scrolls remained in eleven caves for 2,000 years, until they were discovered by three Arab boys who were looking after sheep and goats. One lobbed a stone into a cave, heard a *clonk* and made "the greatest manuscript discovery of modern times" (the description is W. F. Albright's).

A few days later Muhammed edh-Dhib, the youngest of the three, went back to explore and found pots containing leather rolls with writing on. He didn't realise that the scrolls were valuable. Nor did anyone else. For some weeks they remained in a tent. Then some of the scrolls were sold for £24 and £7!

They have become more famous than most archaeo-logical discoveries, partly because some writers have suggested that the scrolls cast doubts upon the origins of the Christian Faith. Three men in particular have popularised this view: André Dupont-Sommer (a French scholar), Edmund Wilson (an American literary critic) and John Allegro (a British scholar).

In a talk on BBC radio, John Allegro suggested that there were strong similarities between Jesus and the origi-nal leader of the Community at Qumran. This man was called the Teacher of Righteousness, and he lived about 100 years before Jesus. Allegro implied that Jesus was not unique, and that Christianity has its roots in the teaching of this Jewish sect, which was flourishing before Jesus was born.

Do the scrolls discredit Jesus?

These novel views were shared by few other scholars. "Nothing that appears in the scrolls hitherto discovered throws any doubt on the originality of Christianity." This sentence was contained in a letter to *The Times* (21st December, 1965). It was signed by eight leading experts in this field. In a book written some years after his broadcast, John Allegro himself admitted that the scrolls do not disprove Christianity.

Work on the scrolls continues, and two Jewish scholars have recently lent their weight to the *un*sensational viewpoint. In his book *The Dead Sea Scrolls*, Geza Vermes does not suggest that they discredit Christianity. True, he does compare Jesus with the Teacher of Righteousness – but only to make the point that Jesus was a much warmer and less austere person. "Jesus . . . appears as a much more human person, whose concern was with other human persons and their need to be taught how to live as the children of God."

Yigael Yadin made a similar point. This remarkable Israeli – soldier, politician and archaeologist – spent his last years studying the longest of the Dead Sea Scrolls (thirty feet). In *The Temple Scroll*, published in 1985 shortly after his death, he states his controversial conclusion that the Qumran religion influenced John the Baptist, St. Paul and St. John.

He also acknowledged that there was a considerable gulf between the Essenes (the name of the tight, austere community which wrote and preserved the scrolls at Qumran), and the early Christians. The Dead Sea Scrolls show an exclusive community, with a rigid adherence to rules. The New Testament shows an open community, well able to adapt. St. Paul's notion that "love is the fulfilling of the law" would be quite unacceptable to his law-dominated neighbours. These differences proved crucial. The Qumran Community died out; the Christian community thrived.

It is because of Jesus' flexible attitude to religious laws (e.g. "the Sabbath was made for man") that Yigael Yadin calls him "anti-Essene". The British scholar Alan Millard would support this. Recently (1985) he wrote: "The differences between the Teacher of Righteousness and Jesus are huge."

If the Dead Sea Scrolls do not discredit Christianity, do they relate to it at all? The answer is "Yes", and I will select four areas.

1. Background information: The Essenes shared a country and a culture with Jesus and his disciples. So the scrolls throw light upon the attitudes, the customs, and the divisions in Palestine during the lifetime of Jesus. In this way they illuminate the background against which many of the events of the New Testament took place.

2. A reliable text: Secondly, they increase our confidence in the reliability of the text of the Bible. At least part of every Old Testament book except one (Esther) has been found in the scrolls. These Scripture passages are in Hebrew – the language in which the Old Testament was originally written. They are much older than any other Hebrew Old Testament texts so far discovered – *about one thousand years older.*

Yet a comparison of those parts of the Bible found in the Dead Sea Scrolls with these other much later copies, shows a striking similarity. There are differences of course – this is inevitable over a period of 1,000 years. But the differences do not affect the sense. The *similarities* far outweigh the differences.

It is clear that over the centuries Jewish communities cherished their Scriptures, and copied them with great care. They did all in their power to keep them pure and unchanged, and they were remarkably successful. Because they are very ancient, the Dead Sea Scrolls provide a yardstick by which we can measure that success. As a result they have *increased* our confidence in the accuracy of the Bible.

Magnus Magnusson, a broadcaster with a special interest

in archaeology, speaks of the "very few minor variations" in the scroll of the Book of Isaiah. He continues: "This underlines the essential integrity of the scribal tradition, that a manuscript could be copied over and over again for a thousand years and still preserve an extremely faithful version of the original."

3. Facts can kill fashions: We have seen that the scrolls have increased our confidence in the text of the Old Testament. What about the New Testament?

At one time it was fashionable among some scholars to assert that the Fourth Gospel was written late in the second century. They asserted that its key ideas were at home in Greek, rather than in Jewish, culture. In the absence of detailed information it was easy to speculate about a late date. Many scholars viewed the Fourth Gospel as a profound meditation written by a Christian of the second century. It was brimful of spiritual value, but had little historical value.

This plausible theory was killed by two specific facts. The first fact was the discovery, in the sands of Egypt, of a papyrus fragment from a copy of St. John's Gospel. This was identified in Manchester in 1934 where it was dated at about AD 130 – pointing to a first-century date for the original.

The second destructive fact was the discovery of the Dead Sea Scrolls. Those who believed that the Fourth Gospel was a free composition written under strong Greek (i.e. Gentile) influence pointed to contrasts drawn by the author. Contrasts like "darkness and light", "good and evil", "life and death". These are *Greek* ideas, they argued, not Jewish. As Jesus was a Jew, the implication was clear. The Gospel was not "earthed" in his life.

Then the scrolls were discovered. They were written by a tightly organised Jewish community. This community rejected all foreign influence – Roman overlords; Greek ideas; everything not thoroughly Jewish.

The text of the scrolls produced some surprises. For one thing, they abound in contrasts – contrasts like darkness and light; good and evil; life and death! It seems that after all, St. John's Gospel fits well into Jewish thought forms which were in use at the time of Jesus. Rather than emphasising Greek influence, some scholars began to suggest that St. John's is the most Jewish of all the Gospels! Others suspected an Aramaic "first-draft" – and Aramaic was the first language of Jesus (although he would almost certainly have spoken Greek too).

4. Beware sensation seekers: Last week I received a postcard from two students who had cycled the length of Britain – 874 miles – to raise money for the fight against Multiple Sclerosis. The postcard shows a group of naked cyclists arriving at Land's End three years earlier. This group wanted to gain publicity for their chosen cause and judged – rightly – that if you cause a sensation, you become well known.

The same principle applies to religious matters. When a Bible scholar says "I believe in Jesus Christ" no one is interested. When a Bible scholar says "I *don't* believe in Jesus Christ" the newspapers are there like a flash.

Careful study of the Dead Sea Scrolls by a host of scholars has *increased* our confidence in the Bible. Yet the views of those few scholars who have tried to use the scrolls to undermine Christianity are more widely known. The student who spoke about the *South* Sea Scrolls shows this very clearly!

No doubt other sensation-stirrers will pick up pens, or sit at word processors, or gather in TV studios, and influence thousands. Christians and serious enquirers will be wise to save their energies for considering criticisms of the Faith with real substance.

CONCLUDING QUOTATIONS

It is my considered conclusion, however, that if one will go through any of the historic statements of Christian faith he will find nothing that has been or can be disproved by the Dead Sea Scrolls – *Professor Millar Burrows (Yale University)*.

If the Isaiah scroll is anything to go by, those who take a high view of the authority of the Bible have nothing to fear, and much to gain, from this research (into the Dead Sea Scrolls). It is a staggering fact that in the course of 1,000 years of copying by hand no errors have crept into the text which in any way affect the Bible teaching – *Alan Millard, Rankin Reader in Hebrew and Ancient Semitic Languages, Liverpool University*.

Note: Alan Millard's fine book *Treasures from Bible Times* is a mine of information about archaeology which relates to the Bible (Lion 1985).

POSTSCRIPT ON SCHOLARS AND SENSATIONS

A backbench MP reminded the House of Commons that the Ark was built by amateurs, and the *Titanic* by professionals. It was an important caution. Beware the expert!

Of course we must listen to scholarly experts, and I have already quoted a fair number. But they are fallible human beings like the rest of us, and they can – and do – make mistakes.

Some scholars are too cautious – unwilling to challenge prevailing academic fashions. Others get their facts wrong or show bad judgment – like the eminent historian who lent his support to the faked "Hitler Diaries". (A few years earlier that same historian attacked the Gospels, and got his facts badly wrong about the dating of the New Testament documents.)

As we have seen, a few scholars love to cause a sensation. Recent books from scholarly pens have suggested the following: that the early Christians were "into" drugs and sex – under cover of the moral teaching of the New Testament; that Jesus took a drug before the crucifixion – gambling that he would come through the ordeal alive; that the geography of the Bible belongs to Arabia not Palestine; that Jesus was invented; that . . .

All this can be very alarming to ordinary Christians who don't know whether a particular sensational viewpoint is widely shared by other experts. Professor James Dunn (himself a scholar!) puts all this into perspective:

> Since Christianity and scholarship share the same passion for truth, Christianity and scholarship are in fact natural allies – common foes of all forms of falsehood, distortion and obscurantism.
>
> So Christianity has nothing to fear from scholarship. Scholars may be a different matter! For individual scholars have their biases and prejudices like every other human being . . . But even so, Christianity need have little fear of such scholars. For scholars have to work from the evidence available to them. And evidence has the happy knack of undermining the overblown or unbalanced edifices built upon it."

So far, so good. The fact remains that scholarly sensations often get wide coverage. *Example:* a few years ago a way-out anti-Christian theory was serialised in the *Sunday Mirror*. The book sold four editions in four months around the world. *First result:* one wealthy scholar. *Second result:* several readers concluded that Christianity is untrue.

Scholarly response: a careful letter of protest from a group of academics of "several Faiths and none". They made it clear that the book was not based on sound

evidence. Predictably, the letter was sent to *The Times* –
and was not read by most people who buy the *Sunday
Mirror. Concluding plea:* will sane scholars (i.e. the vast
majority) make an effort to communicate with us ordinary
folk, please?

TAKE A BREAK (4)

Let there be light
The Church Business meeting moved to Item 5 on the
Agenda: It read: "Purchase of Candelabra". One long-
standing member stood up – a man who occasionally got
hold of the wrong end of the stick. "I'm against this idea,"
he declared. "For one thing, we have just overhauled the
organ. For another thing, no one in the church can play a
candelabra. In any case, if we have any spare funds, we
should concentrate on improving the lighting in the
church."

* * *

He who laughs last . . .
A new church was to be built. The minister and the
congregation sat down with the architect and hammered
out the design. Then the architect said, "Good, we seem to
be agreed upon most things. There is just one more point. It
is my practice when designing churches to ask the minister
to include one surprise item, and the congregation to
include another."

The great day arrived and the church was to be opened.
The first few folk came in, and to their great surprise, found
only one pew. To their delight it was right at the back,
where everyone loves to sit. But no sooner had they sat
down than the pew rolled smoothly to the front, and
another pew popped up in its place. This was repeated until
the church was full.

The minister was delighted at his surprise item, as he had

the only church in the world which fills up from the front first. He was in such a good mood that enthusiasm carried him away as he preached. Then, exactly fifteen minutes into his sermon, a trap door opened in the pulpit, and he disappeared from sight.

* * *

Two more bishop stories (the last two, I promise)
The bishop had a terrible memory for names. At a residential conference he met one of his clergy. "How is your wife?" he asked. "I'm afraid she died last year, my Lord," was the quiet response. Two days later he met the same man, but – alas – did not recognise him. "How is your wife?" he asked again.

"Still dead, my Lord" came the crisp reply.

* * *

A Victorian bishop was met at the railway station by a horse and trap. As the pony trotted towards the church where the Confirmation Service was to be held, it loosed wind – as only horses can. The horseman was very embarrassed. "Oh, I'm terribly sorry, my Lord," he spluttered. "Not at all," replied the bishop, heartily. "If you hadn't been so honest, I'd have thought it was the horse."

11

MORE ARCHAEOLOGY
AND ITS IMPLICATIONS

Archaeologists working on Biblical sites are keen to explain the nature of their task. They aren't – directly anyway – in the "proof business"; they are concerned with *knowledge*. That is to say, they go to a site to discover what it "says", rather than to prove or disprove the Bible narrative.

They also point out that archaeology, by its very nature, will never be able to answer all our questions – and that it will raise some problems. The spade, the trowel and the sophisticated back-up technology (e.g., determining dates by comparing radioactive carbon with ordinary carbon) often yield incomplete evidence. This is inevitable because archaeologists depend upon a combination of intelligent detective work and happy accident. Archaeology is silent on many questions because the great mass of ancient buildings, walls, tombs and documents have long since been destroyed by damp, or by fire, wind and rain.

With these important cautions, we can confidently say that Biblical archaeology does two things: it demonstrates the need for a "robust" faith, and it shows that such faith is based on sound information.

A robust faith

Some critics of the Christian Faith want too much evidence. Unless every question is answered in full, they refuse to believe. Conversely, some Christians are too concerned to dot every i and cross every t. They have a "domino" view of the Faith. They are terrified that if one item of evidence is hit sideways, this will eventually knock down the whole building.

Neither approach is compatible with strong Christian faith. C. S. Lewis once declared that Christianity is not a "filleted" religion. In other words, it comes to us with "bones" in – with loose ends and problems. To some extent it is untidy. Archaeology illustrates this.

Take Jericho, for example. Under Joshua the Israelites marched round that city seven times, and "the walls came tumbling down" (Josh. 6:20). In the 1930s John Garstang of Liverpool University led a team of excavators to Jericho. They found wall stumps and masses of mud bricks. Once more, archaeology had "proved" the Bible. But in 1952, Kathleen Kenyon and her team reopened the quest. She found that Garstang had been mistaken; the flattened walls were in fact about 1,000 years older than he thought. Then Yigael Yadin entered the debate, and disputed Kathleen Kenyon's interpretation of the evidence.

It would be wrong to infer that Kathleen Kenyon

disproved the Bible account. In fact, she found part of a building which – together with items of pottery – show that Jericho was inhabited around the time of Joshua's attack (1250 BC). Time and erosion have destroyed other possible clues. The evidence raises questions for the Biblical account, but it neither proves nor disproves its accuracy. In this, as in many other matters, we have to live with uncertainty. Disappointing but true.

Confirmation of faith

A robust faith does not worry too much about dotting i's and crossing t's. Men and women with this kind of faith can live with uncertainties, because their faith is built on solid foundations. Such a faith accepts the silence of archaeological evidence on some issues, and the puzzles which it poses for others. But the Bible is a vital part of this solid foundation, and such Christians are not indifferent to evidence – archaeological or otherwise.

In the last chapter we saw that the Dead Sea Scrolls have increased our confidence in both the Old and New Testaments. So far in this chapter I have sounded a cautionary note. I want now to draw attention to a few of the many other archaeological discoveries – in addition to the scrolls – which have confirmed the Bible at many points.

1. Firstly, a word of encouragement from the Bible to those involved in the Channel Tunnel! "It was King Hezekiah who blocked the upper outlet of the Gihon spring and channelled the water down to the west side of the City of David" (2 Chr. 32:30). We know that this is true because it is possible to walk the length of the tunnel – 534 metres – today. Two groups of workmen started digging at each end, and met in the middle in 701 BC.

2. Until recently, we knew about the Roman governor Pontius Pilate only from the New Testament, and from the writings of Josephus, Philo and Tacitus. In 1961 an Italian archaeological expedition working at Caesarea (about 65 miles from Jerusalem) discovered a stone slab.

This was inscribed with three names including those of Pilate and of the Emperor Tiberius.

3. In the Acts of the Apostles we read that Gallio was proconsul of Greece (18:12). An inscription discovered at Delphi records a decision made by Emperor Claudius on a matter referred to him by Gallio. From this, historians deduce that Gallio almost certainly began his term of office in the summer of AD 51. This discovery is important because it provides an accurate reference point for fixing other dates. It is one of a large number of details in Acts which have been shown to be correct.

4. Jesus was brought up in Nazareth in the area of Galilee. We are so familiar with the phrase "Jesus of Nazareth" that it comes as a surprise to find that the town of Nazareth is not mentioned in the Old Testament. Some scholars believed the term "Jesus of Nazareth" to be incorrect, even though it is applied to Jesus in the New Testament. They preferred the term "Nazir*ite*" which *is* found in the Old Testament, and refers to an office, not a place.

Excavations in 1955 demonstrated that a town called Nazareth did, after all, exist in Galilee well before the time of Jesus. Commenting on this, Canon Anthony Harvey writes: "This little episode by no means stands alone. It is symptomatic of the way in which archaeology has tended in recent years to enhance the credibility of the Gospel narratives."

5. In 1968 the bones of a crucified man called Jehohanan were discovered. The nail through his feet was still in place, together with fragments of olive-wood. The bones of his lower leg had been broken. These harrowing details agree entirely with the Gospel accounts of crucifixion.

6. We have already noted that the oldest existing portion of the New Testament is a fragment from St. John's Gospel. This papyrus scrap (containing what we now call John 18: 31–33) was preserved in the dry sands of Egypt for nearly 2,000 years. We also saw that the Dead Sea Scrolls have

illuminated the historical background of St. John's account. As this is often regarded as the least historical of the four Gospels, it is worth noting that some of its details have been verified by archaeology.

For example, the most recent edition of the *Oxford Bible Atlas* (1984) confirms that two important sites have been located by archaeologists. These are the pools of Bethesda (John 5:2) and Siloam (John 9:7), where Jesus is said to have performed healing miracles.

Professor A. M. Hunter sums up: "Thus archaeological discovery has, at point after point, tended to confirm John's topography, even if all problems have not been finally solved."

7. The Temple which Jesus visited, and in which he taught, was destroyed in AD 70 when the Romans crushed the Jewish rebellion. Little of it remains, but there are two items worth noting.

Firstly, the massive stones which can now be seen in Jerusalem's famous "Wailing Wall". Some of these survived the Roman attack. They are from the huge platform which supported the Temple, not from the Temple itself. The largest stone block measures 16½ feet by 13 feet.

Secondly, a notice engraved in limestone, discovered in 1871. This stone slab measures about 2 feet by 3 feet and illuminates various Bible passages. Part of a second, similar notice was found in 1936. Investigation showed that the letters were originally painted red (appropriate, as we shall see!).

In Acts 21 Luke describes a riot which began when Paul was accused of taking a Greek friend into the Temple. No wonder! Here is the inscription on the stone: *No foreigner may pass the barrier and enclosure surrounding the Temple. Anyone who is caught doing so will be himself to blame for his resulting death*.

Paul denied the charge. He knew that Gentiles could go so far – and no further. In his letter to the Ephesians, Paul reminded his readers that Jesus has broken down the wall which once divided Jews and Gentiles. Those who know about the famous Jerusalem Temple, with its sequence of barriers, would readily understand this teaching.

I am tempted to multiply examples. I want to write about Ahab's palace of ivory; about the clay tablets from Ugarit which illustrate the nature religion of Canaan, against which the Israelites were constantly warned; about the three chariot cities of Solomon; about the amazing engineering feats of Herod the Great (or, more accurately, Herod the horrible); about . . . But I must be disciplined! So I will end with a summary, and then let the experts speak for themselves.

Summary
The list of archaeological discoveries which relate to the Bible is impressive. Difficulties remain, of course. There are still many points where our knowledge about people, places, and dates is incomplete or confused.

In any case, archaeological evidence is *indirect* evidence. It demonstrates that at many points the Bible is historically reliable. It provides information which helps us to understand customs and attitudes in Bible times. But it cannot prove or disprove the truth of Christianity. And it certainly cannot prove or disprove the existence of God.

What it *does* show is that we may approach the Bible with confidence. When we add to this the evidence for the New Testament text outlined earlier, our confidence grows. As the Bible is basic material for the Christian Faith, this is an extremely important first step.

CONCLUDING QUOTATIONS

. . . it is a fact that, by and large, modern archaeological science has done a great deal to confirm the accuracy of the history recorded in the Bible, and only rarely and in relatively unimportant matters does it put a question mark against the biblical record – *Professor I. Howard Marshall*.

. . . it may be stated categorically that no archaeological discovery has ever controverted a biblical reference – *Professor Nelson Glueck – one-time President of the Hebrew Union College Biblical and Archaeological School*.

There can be no doubt that archaeology has confirmed the substantial historicity of the Old Testament tradition – *Professor W. F. Albright*.

Archaeology has indeed corroborated the substantial historicity of the Biblical record from the patriarchal period to the apostolic age, but it is not by archaeology that the essential message of the Bible can be verified. Sometimes . . . indeed, archaeology has made the interpretation of the Biblical narrative more difficult rather than less so – *Professor F. F. Bruce*.

So far, archaeology has really only scratched the surface, metaphorically speaking. But with every month and every year, new archaeological discoveries are lighting up our knowledge and our understanding of the Bible lands BC – *Magnus Magnusson*.

12

TOO VIOLENT, TOO OLD, TOO CONTRADICTORY

At the end of this section of questions about the Bible, we shall look briefly at three further objections.

A violent book
This cannot be disputed. The ancient world was a violent world. Fighting between nations was universal, and Israel was no exception. Many battles are described in the Bible, and the Israelites prayed for God's help as they fought.

But the Israelites were different from their neighbours in many ways. They knew that certain forms of violence were forbidden – human sacrifice for example. And their teachers and prophets emphasised the importance of offering care and hospitality – especially to orphans, to widows, and to foreigners within their borders.

Two further points are relevant. *Firstly*, the Bible is an honest book. It refuses to whitewash its heroes. The cowardice of Peter is not hushed up. But it is not recorded as an example to be copied. In the same way, the violence of David, and of the poet who wrote Psalm 137, are there for all to see. But they are condemned by the very scriptures which so honestly describe these human failings.

Secondly, the Bible shows moral and spiritual development. I am not suggesting that we find a smooth progression from violence to love. The upward path was very uneven, and some Old Testament characters were streets ahead of many in the New Testament, or in the modern world.

But development there is. Slowly, over the centuries, God taught them more about love and forgiveness. The climax came when Jesus told his astonished hearers: "Love your enemies." He put his own teaching into practice. On the cross he prayed for his torturers: "Father, forgive them, for they do not know what they are doing."

An old book

The Bible is about people whose transport was limited to horses and camels (or feet!) over land, and wind in sails or oars across water. How can it have anything relevant to say to a generation which can get to the moon?

If we concentrate on surface differences – clothes, customs, travel – we shall see ourselves as totally different from the men and women we read about in the Bible. Logical conclusion? That the Bible has nothing useful to say to the modern world.

Certainly, we should not underestimate the differences: in many ways their attitudes and assumptions were *very* different from ours. Quite often we need to probe hard into that world, before we can make good sense of the Bible.

But the *similarities* between Bible characters and ourselves are enormous too. The problems they faced were basically our problems: the cost of living, war and peace, getting on with other people, making sense of life. We find in the Bible people who fell in love, people who hated, people who were anxious and afraid, people who worked, people who laughed and cried, people who became ill, people who grew old, people who died.

The Bible is about men and women like that, and about activities like that. It deals with the "constants" in human life, and it deals with them in a profound way.

It was a book for the first century. It is a book for the twentieth century. It is a book for all ages.

Full of contradiction and error

It will be obvious from earlier chapters that I don't agree with this objection, for I have a high view of the Bible's reliability. I readily agree that we must read the Bible intelligently – accepting the different kinds of writing (history, poetry, parable, law, etc.) for what they are. And I readily accept that any library of sixty-six books written by authors and editors over a thousand-or-so years, is likely to contain many differences of viewpoint and approach. Indeed, it is the overall *unity* of the Bible's message which impresses me, not any apparent errors and contradictions.

But nothing is gained by pretending that problems don't exist.

Some religions protect their holy books from close critical scrutiny. For example, Muslims and Mormons claim that the Qur'ān and the Book of Mormon came directly from God – by dictation and by tablets respectively. In contrast, the full human involvement of the writers of the Bible is freely acknowledged by Christians. We believe that God's Spirit guided those men as they wrote, by using – not bypassing – their personalities, gifts, and experiences. God certainly didn't tidy up Mark's rough Greek style! This is an *encouragement*, not a problem, for it shows that God can use us – warts and all.

However, while I do believe that God inspired and guided the writers, I haven't tried to prove this. I have attempted something more modest – to demonstrate that the Bible (especially the Gospels) is sufficiently accurate and reliable for us to take it seriously.

As stated earlier (page 109), my concern is for a robust faith – a faith which can face problems and live with untidiness. This is such an important point that I will close by describing two believers who have found error and contradiction in the Scriptures. They didn't pretend. They didn't despair. They acknowledged the difficulties, but kept them in perspective. For their faith was, and is, built on solid foundations, which can't be shaken by small details.

John Calvin, the great sixteenth-century Reformer, had a very high view of the Bible, and he wrote long books of exposition. In Matt. 27:9 the Evangelist quotes the Prophet Jeremiah. Calvin knew the Old Testament so well that he recognised this to be an error. He commented: "I confess I do not know how the 'Jeremiah' came in here, and I do not worry much. Certainly it is an obvious mistake to put Jeremiah for Zechariah, for we do not find anything like it in Jeremiah." He then proceeded to write thousands more words of Bible exposition. This small point did not in the least disturb his belief in the Bible as the Word of God.

A modern example comes from the pen of Professor Howard Marshall of Aberdeen University. Mark and Matthew give rather different accounts of the healing of Blind Bartimaeus (Mark 10:46–52; Matt. 20:29–34). In Mark there is one blind man; in Matthew there are two. Professor Marshall comments: "It seems probable that Matthew has doubled the numbers without any historical basis in the stories themselves; it is possible that he was trying to indicate that Jesus performed more healings of the same kind than he had space to record as separate incidents."

This does not shake his belief in the overall reliability of the Gospel accounts. This is shown by the title of the book from which I have quoted: *I Believe in the Historical Jesus* (1977). Nor does it disturb his view of the Bible as inspired Scripture. Later, he wrote a book entitled *The Inspiration of the Bible*. He concludes this by movingly describing the basis of his own faith: "It is through the Bible that I know of the God who has declared his salvation in the life, death and resurrection of Jesus, and with deepest thankfulness I embrace that saving truth and stake my life on it."

Note: After writing this chapter I looked up Matthew 27:9 in the scholarly *Peake's Commentary*. The writer agrees that the quotation is from Zechariah, but he adds "with certain allusions to Jeremiah 18:2–3 and 36:6–15". So perhaps Matthew wasn't quite as wrong as Calvin supposed!

Part IV

Questions about Suffering

My God, my God, why have you forsaken me?
Psalm 22:1 and Mark 15:34

It was only when I lay there on rotting prison straw that I sensed within myself the first stirring of good. Gradually it was disclosed to me that the line separating Good and Evil passes, not through States, not between classes, not between political parties either – but right through every human heart – and through all human hearts . . . And that is why I turn back to the years of my imprisonment and say, sometimes to the astonishment of those about me: "*Bless you*, prison!"
Alexander Solzhenitsyn

13

WHY DOES GOD ALLOW SUFFERING?

As I write, the world news is bleak. Three plane crashes, and three train crashes, have recently killed hundreds. Wars flare up; civil wars drag on. Nature continues "red in tooth and claw". A terrible earthquake dominates the headlines. Hundreds – possibly thousands – dead. And some amazing escapes.

The news has been lightened a little by the generous giving of many ordinary people to combat hunger. But even this has reminded us of continuing famine in Africa. The grim words of Jesus have again been grimly fulfilled: "For nation will rise against nation, and kingdom against kingdom. There will be famines and earthquakes in various places" (Matt. 24:7).

Life isn't all gloom and doom however. I have just been given a paperback entitled *Chase* in which a policeman describes his narrow escape from death. A bullet hit his teeth, and the tough enamel ("a kind of organic steel") deflected it. He believes that God saved his life.

On a lighter note, a letter in the *Church Times* describes the breakdown of a family car, followed by a child's question: "Why don't we pray about it?" Rather embarrassed, they did. And – you've guessed it – help arrived. Next week, the predictable questions were raised. Why should God answer *that* prayer in that way? Isn't that favouritism? Ethiopian believers pray too; where is God's bounty then?

Well, we have it on the highest authority that God *does* have a preference for childlike prayers. But the questioners have a point too. Surely some of the Ethiopian believers are children. Why, then, is God silent? (*Stop press*: the latest news from East Africa is a little more heartening. So perhaps after all . . .)

But still the question persists. Why does God allow such terrible things to happen? This is the most difficult question of all, for any person who believes in an all-loving and all-powerful God. Is there an answer?

Certainly there is no easy answer, but this does not mean that we can say nothing. As we consider the problem it becomes clear that the fact of suffering raises, not one, but *two* theological questions – as well as a host of practical questions about effective action.

First question: Why does God allow these things to happen? *Second question:* Does God really care for us? Indeed, is he really there at all? We will look at each of these in turn.

1. Why?
Why does God allow such things to happen?

The short answer is – we simply do not know. When we consider why this particular accident happened, or why that particular child died so young, we are forced to admit that we can give no answer. This becomes especially difficult in the light of claims by other people that God *did* step in and help them.

We find important clues in the Bible. Jesus himself accepted suffering as an inescapable ingredient of life. He made it clear that we must never assume that personal disaster is God's punishment for personal sin (Luke 13: 1–5). Certainly we must never act as judge in such matters. That is God's work, not ours.

Time and again Jesus repeated the phrase: "Don't be afraid". He wasn't an escapist. He didn't pretend that the sky is always blue. He lived in a cruel and dangerous world which eventually crucified him. But he knew that we are never abandoned by God – even though we may sometimes *feel* abandoned. Even death itself is not the final disaster which we imagine it to be.

Further clues can be found in the book of Genesis. We read there about the rebellion of the first human beings against the will of God. This "Fall of Man" affected – for the worse – the world in which we live. But this is not easy to understand, and those who do not accept a Christian view of the world, will – understandably – not readily accept this notion.

Even if the ultimate answer to the problem of suffering is to be found along these lines, our investigations will not take us that far. Our problem is more immediate. Why *this* earthquake? Why did God allow *that* accident? Reluctantly we admit that, usually, we can give no answer.

We need to remember, however, that to say that we do not know the reason is quite different from saying that there is no reason. When my television set went wrong, I had no idea why it gave a thin bright band instead of a picture. But I was quite sure that a reason existed, which is why I sent for a television engineer.

2. Does God care?

Behind the question *Why?* stands this further question. We have an uneasy feeling that the God who allows these things to happen may not really care for us – if he exists at all.

Does God exist? Is he indifferent? Or does God love the world which he has created? Here we can give a clear and definite answer, for we have clear and definite evidence. Yes, God *does* love us. We know this because he has given us a clear demonstration of his love. *He sent his Son to die for us.*

At first, this might seem to be a rather slick answer. In fact, it is the greatest of all answers, to the greatest of all questions. It is the keynote of the New Testament. Does God love us? To this question the Bible replies: "For God so loved the world that he gave his only Son" (John 3:16, RSV).

Here, as always, it is the person of Jesus who makes sense of life. The fact of Christ is the answer to the problem of suffering.

This is supported by another kind of evidence – the fact that people often speak of experiencing the strength of God *in and through* their suffering. Bishop Leonard Wilson was taken prisoner during the Second World War. He was tortured, and his tormentors taunted him: You believe in God. Why doesn't he save you? The bishop replied that God did save him – not by removing the pain, but by giving him the strength to bear it.

After the war, he confirmed a man whose face seemed familiar. He realised that the man had been one of his interrogators. The bishop's faith as he suffered had convinced that man of the reality of Christ.

The balance principle

Very often life demands that we "weigh" facts. A friend is accused of theft. There is evidence which appears to be against him. He was outside the supermarket with some items in his bag – items which he hadn't paid for.

What can we put on the other side of the balance? We *know* our friend. All our experience of him suggests that he is honest. We know that when he found fifty pounds, he handed it to the police.

The fact that he was found with the goods presents a problem for our faith in our friend. Against this evidence, we balance our personal knowledge of him. Then we decide which way the balance must come down.

GUILTY

OUR KNOWL-EDGE OF OUR FRIEND

EVIDENCE AGAINST

EVIDENCE AGAINST

OUR KNOWL-EDGE OF OUR FRIEND

NOT GUILTY

Of course, we may suspect that our friend is basically *dis*honest – in which case there is nothing we can put on the right-hand side. It is not the details which matter here, but the way in which we tackle a problem like this.

This balance principle provides the key to the solution of the problem which pain and suffering present for our belief in God. We must insist on looking at *all* of the evidence. The atheist will draw our attention to part of the evidence – the fact of suffering. We must take this into account. Certainly it weighs heavily on the left-hand side of the balance.

But we must also take into account the fact of Jesus Christ, and the not uncommon experience of unexpected strength in suffering. This too is evidence. If it is true that God sent his Son, and that he continues to send his Spirit, because he loves us, then this tips the scale. Two further illustrations will make the issues clearer.

1. An imaginary war story: During the last war Mr. Brown was involved with the French Resistance movement. He was introduced to M. Defarge who, he was told, was head of the whole operation. They worked together and Mr. Brown was tremendously impressed with M. Defarge.

On one occasion they planned to blow up an ammunition store. It was almost certain that those who took part would die. Defarge's son volunteered, and with much grief Defarge allowed him to go. The mission was successful but his son was killed.

One day Defarge told Brown that they must alter their tactics. He warned Brown that he would see him doing things which he would not understand. On occasions, Brown saw Defarge helping their own men to escape. At other times Brown saw him standing by while their men were handed over to the Nazis. Sometimes Defarge even appeared in the uniform of the enemy. "He is a traitor!" cried Brown's comrades.

But Brown knew Defarge. In particular, he knew that he had allowed his son to die for the cause. Because of this, Brown was convinced that he could be trusted. He was often bewildered, but he knew that although he could not understand, there must be a reason. At last, the war was over. Brown and Defarge met once more, and Defarge explained why he did those things which at the time were so bewildering.

The atheist is in the position of Brown's comrades. He considers only part of the evidence – the fact of suffering.

The Christian is like Brown. He is often bewildered by occurrences which he cannot understand. His faith is sorely tried by terrible events which suggest that God does not care. But he knows God. Above all he knows that God sent his Son to die for us. It is because of this that he is certain that God loves us.

2. An incident from the mission field: This time we are dealing with fact. John Paton was a Christian missionary. In 1858 he and his young pregnant wife went to the primitive Island of Tanna in the New Hebrides. During the first year she died of fever. This was followed seventeen days later by the death of their one-month-old son. Grief-stricken, John Paton buried his wife and child. He recorded these words:

> It was very difficult to be resigned, left alone, and in sorrowful circumstances; but feeling immovably assured that my God and Father was too wise and loving to err in anything that He does or permits, I looked up to the Lord for help, and struggled on in His work. I do not pretend to see through the mystery of such visitations – wherein God calls away the young, the promising, and those sorely needed for His service here; but this I do know and feel, that, in the light of such dispensations, it becomes us all to love and serve our blessed Lord Jesus so that we may be ready at His call for death and Eternity.

Notice: "I do not pretend to see through the mystery . . ." To the question *Why?* he could give no answer. No doubt he prayed that God – the source of all love and power – would step in to heal. He could not understand why he did not do so. But to our second question – *does God care?* – John Paton affirmed that God is a Father who loves.

This is the authentic voice of faith. *The person with a living faith is often bewildered, but he is prepared to live with questions which he cannot answer, in the light of the great answers which he* does *possess.*

Such faith is not a blind refusal to face the facts. Rather, it comes from a concern to take into account *all* the facts: the fact of suffering *and* the fact of Christ. Such faith is not based on a refusal to consider the evidence. Indeed it springs from a refusal to leave out that part of the evidence which non-Christians so often ignore – the evidence of God's love shown by the fact that he sent his Son and that he continues to strengthen us by his Spirit.

But all this raises another big question. Is the coming of Jesus Christ into our world a fact of sufficient importance to weigh down the scales? Clearly the whole solution depends on this. Is Jesus *that* significant? We shall turn to this question next. But before we do so, two other brief but important points.

1. Suffering and the Cross of Christ

A few years ago I was interested in buying a print based on a Russian icon. Proceeds from the sale would help Christians in Eastern Europe, and I am moved by some Russian art, so it seemed a happy combination. Then I read the description. The picture showed Jesus in Glory. He was strong and serene – apparently above, and untouched by, the sufferings of the world.

I decided not to buy that picture after all. No doubt the picture conveyed deep truths about the vindication and glorification of Jesus. But it seemed to me to distort the meaning of the Cross.

Jesus is no mere spectator to the anguish of the world. He understands it *from the inside*. He is able to sympathise with our weakness, because he was tempted. He is able to enter into our suffering, because he too has suffered. We are required to forgive those who harm us, because he forgives us.

And if this suggests a sympathetic Son of God, and an indifferent God, let us recall that fathers suffer in the anguish of their children. "God was in Christ reconciling the world to himself" (2 Cor. 5:19, RSV).

2. Suffering and weakness

Some people triumph over pain and tragedy with a glowing and untroubled faith. But it isn't always like that. St. Paul wrote to the Church at Corinth "out of much affliction and anguish of heart and with many tears". And the shortest verse in the Bible is amongst the most moving: "Jesus wept" (John 11:35).

It is clear that we are sometimes called to share our *weakness*, rather than our strength.

I recall a friend whose wife died when he was a curate. They had three young children and he attempted to keep the family routine as steady as possible. He went shopping and the tears flowed. He felt an abject failure.

Here was a marvellous opportunity to encourage his parishioners with the strength of his faith – and all he could do was cry! Later he came to see that his tears encouraged them more than his strength would have done. He began to understand what St. Paul meant when he said that God's strength "is made perfect in weakness" (2 Cor. 12:9).

CONCLUDING QUOTATION

People used continually to ask us why a young man of such promise, and with such a zest for life, should be allowed to die so young. To this the only reply, we both feel, is that we do not, and cannot, know. The vital question to ask God in such cases is not, "Why did you allow this?" (to which he seldom, I think, vouchsafes an answer), but, "What do you want to teach me through this?" – *Professor Sir Norman Anderson*.

(This quotation is from his recent autobiography: *An Adopted Son*. I describe the background to this moving passage on page 159.)

Part V

Questions about Jesus

I believe there is no one lovelier, deeper, more sympathetic and more perfect than Jesus . . . not only is there no one else like him, but there could never be any one like him.

Fyodor Dostoyevsky

Something absolutely marvellous happened in Galilee 2,000 years ago.

Alec McCowen

The Christ of the Christians is a quite concrete, human, historical person: the Christ of the Christians is no other than *Jesus of Nazareth*.

Hans Küng

14

WAS JESUS INVENTED?

Christ was born about seven years before Christ. This remarkable fact is not due to a major miracle; it is due to a minor miscalculation. The fact that the calculation was made at all *is* a miracle.

The odds against that particular baby becoming so famous must be a trillion, trillion, trillion to one. Nevertheless, it remains true that several hundred years after his death this village carpenter had become so important that it was decided to date the calendar with reference to his birth. But his birth was so obscure that they got the dates wrong!

Christians rejoice in Jesus' humble origins. And we

rejoice that it was *after* his death that he made an impact on the world outside Palestine. We rejoice, for this convinces us of the reality of the resurrection (see Chapter 16).

But these facts present problems too. Roman politicians and historians were not interested in a young carpenter turned preacher. They began to sit up and take notice only when the dust began to settle in Palestine – and to blow around elsewhere in the Empire. This didn't happen until some years after his execution.

As a result there is a great deal that we *don't* know about Jesus. We don't even know the colour of his eyes, his height and weight, or whether he was good-looking, ugly, or just plain ordinary. Countless artists and film directors have tried to fill *that* particular vacuum!

Because of this time gap, it is possible to speculate as to whether Jesus really existed. Perhaps his followers invented him – though it would be inaccurate to call them "followers" if they had!

During the last two centuries, some scholars have argued for this. And in the Soviet Union today, children are taught that Jesus was a second-century invention. He was invented, they say, to account for an early Communist movement.

Significantly, few recent historians have gone down that road. So Professor W. D. Davies could say: "The existence of Jesus as a historical figure is not now seriously questioned." Another scholar – C. J. Cadoux – put it even more strongly: "The idea is quite fantastic, and has not been championed, so far as I know, by any competent historian."

But recently those judgments have been challenged by G. A. Wells, an English professor of German. He argues that Jesus was the product of the imagination of St. Paul and his fellow Christians.

In any case, the idea that Jesus didn't really exist surfaces from time to time in conversations about Christianity, so the need to produce evidence cannot be ducked. This evidence has three separate strands.

A. Evidence from ancient non-Christian sources

Because space is limited and this information is readily available elsewhere (see page 143), I will not attempt to give a full account of the evidence from ancient non-Christian sources. But I will make three points:

1. A taster: To give you a taste of the evidence – and the problems which accompany it – I will set out a famous quotation from the Jewish historian Josephus, who was born about AD 37. He defected to the Romans in the Jewish–Roman war which started in AD 66, and which is referred to in the Gospels. Josephus mentions Jesus in two passages in his famous *Antiquities*. Here is the longer of the two:

> Now, there was about this time Jesus, a wise man, *if it be lawful to call him a man*, for he was a doer of wonderful works, a teacher of such men as receive the truth with pleasure. He drew over to him both many of the Jews, and many of the Gentiles. *He was (the) Christ.* And when Pilate, at the suggestion of the principal men amongst us, had condemned him to the cross, those that loved him at the first did not forsake him; *for he appeared to them alive again at the third day; as the divine prophets had foretold these and ten thousand other wonderful things concerning him.* And the tribe of Christians, so named from him, are not extinct at this day.

I have put some sentences in italics because many scholars believe these to be later Christian insertions. But most scholars believe the rest to be authentic, for there is no textual evidence against either of Josephus' "Jesus passages".

2. The importance of what the Rabbis didn't *say.* From

the Tannaitic period of Jewish history (AD 70–200) we
have a few references to Jesus. By this time Jews and
Christians were in dispute, and it would have suited Jewish
teachers to be able to cast doubt upon the existence of
Jesus. They did not do so.

Quite the reverse. In the Jewish Talmud Jesus is acknowledged as a Jew, and described as an executed false teacher.
His miracles, teachings and disciples are all referred to.
Professor F. F. Bruce sums up: "The rabbis of this period,
then, were not unacquainted with the story of Jesus and the
activity of his followers, vigorously as they voiced their
dissent from all that he and they stood for."

3. *There is more evidence for Christians than for Christ.*
Those Roman officials and historians who took an interest
in the Christian movement did so reluctantly. For the word
Christian seemed to be spelt T-R-O-U-B-L-E. So Pliny the
Younger (Roman Governor of Bithynia: AD 110–113),
Suetonius (a Roman historian who wrote around AD 100),
and Tacitus (a Roman historian born in AD 56) were more
interested in the antics – as they regarded them – of the
early Christians than in Jesus himself. But they did not
doubt that behind it all was a man called Christ (or Chrestus
or Christos). For example, in his *Annals* Tacitus describes
how the Emperor Nero used the Christians as a scapegoat
for the burning of Rome.

> Therefore, to scotch the rumours, Nero substituted as
> culprits, and punished with the utmost of cruelty, a class
> of men, loathed for their vices, whom the crowd styled
> Christians (*Christianos*). Christus, the founder of the
> name, had undergone the death penalty in the reign
> of Tiberius, by sentence of the procurator Pontius
> Pilate . . .

Of course, Tacitus never met Jesus. He knew about Jesus
from the Christians of his day – and perhaps from another
important source too. As Professor Bruce points out,

Tacitus enjoyed high status, and might have had access to official Roman records.

To sum up: I readily acknowledge that we do not have vast quantities of detailed information about Jesus from these early non-Christian sources. In the nature of the case we would not expect this. It was only when the Christian movement would not lie down – despite slander, scorn and persecution – that politicians and historians began to take notice.

On the basis of the evidence we do have, we can be quite sure of two things. *Firstly*, that Jesus existed. *Secondly*, that he was a notable teacher, that he gained a reputation as a miracle worker, that he offended authority, and that he was executed.

The evidence for these points from non-Christian sources is supported by two other sets of data.

B. Early Christian evidence
In addition to the inevitably sparse comments from Roman and Jewish sources we have a large quantity of early Christian material. In particular, we have the Gospels. I shall not repeat my reasons for believing them to give a substantially accurate account of the life of Jesus (see Chapters 9–12). But I will make three points.

Firstly: many of the finest, most detailed studies of great people have come from their friends or followers – for example, Boswell on Johnson and Plato on Socrates. Of course, we make allowances for bias. But we also recognise that close friends are the only people who have detailed, accurate information.

Secondly: the Gospels were a totally new and unique form of literature. *Something* happened in first-century Palestine which produced an unparalleled burst of joyful, creative energy. Everything about the Gospels suggests that they were *inspired by someone* (or *Someone*), not cooked up by clever inventors.

Professor C. S. Lewis immersed himself in literature of

all kinds. Writing about St. John's Gospel he gave this
judgment:

> Either this is reportage – though it may no doubt contain
> errors – pretty close up to the facts; . . . Or else, some
> unknown writer in the second century, without known
> predecessors or successors, suddenly anticipated the
> whole technique of modern, novelistic, realistic narra-
> tive. If it is untrue, it must be narrative of that kind. The
> reader who doesn't see this has simply not learned to
> read.

Lewis makes it clear that the first possibility has all of his
votes.

Thirdly: if the men who produced the Gospels were
inventors, they were incredibly subtle – building in a
complicated range of difficulties – or very hamfisted as
historians. Brilliant inventors would have included a few
problems, of course – but they would not have risked so
many loose ends and unresolved questions. Some of those
notorious differences between the Gospels would certainly
have been ironed out! The fact they did not do a tidier job
strongly suggests that the Gospel writers were faithful to
their sources and to their memories.

Don Cupitt and Peter Armstrong make this point in *Who
Was Jesus?*

> If the Gospels are myth dressed up as historical fact, then
> the job has not been done very well . . . If a myth is being
> projected back into history, why this bit of history, and
> why create needless difficulties?

C. Modern witnesses
This brings me to the third and final strand in the evidence
for the reality of the historical Jesus. He is "solid" enough

to make a tremendous impression upon a wide range of people in our century. Here are a few examples.

A Communist. In the 1970s a Czech, Milan Machoveč, wrote *A Marxist Looks at Jesus*. He acknowledged that Jesus "set the world on fire", and he explains why: ". . . he himself was the attraction. They saw in him a man who already belonged to this coming Kingdom of God; they saw what it meant to be 'full of grace' . . ."

Two Jewish scholars. Geza Vermes is a Jewish scholar based in Oxford. He warmly acknowledges Jesus as a fellow Jew who was "an unsurpassed master of the art of laying bare the inmost core of spiritual truth".

Martin Buber, a great Jewish leader of our century, goes as far as a Jew can, without actually becoming a Christian! "From my youth onwards I have found in Jesus my great brother . . . I am more than ever certain that a great place belongs to him in Israel's history of faith and that this place cannot be described by any of the usual categories."

A famous Hindu. It is said that Mahatma Gandhi had a crucifix in his office, and that "When I Survey the Wondrous Cross" was his favourite hymn. Of Jesus he said: "I believe that he belongs not only to Christianity but to the entire world, to all races and people."

Two scholarly sceptics. Don Cupitt is a dean who delights in doubt. He encourages scepticism, and loves to stir a theological scandal. In *Who Was Jesus?* (written with Peter Armstrong) he warns us not to accept the Gospels as a simple, straightforward record. Despite this he speaks highly of St. Luke's integrity as a historian. And he does not doubt the existence of the historical Jesus:

> We can't promise too much . . . But we suggest that the main themes of his life and teaching can be recovered. Enough does emerge to give us plenty to think about . . . So there is every reason to think that Jesus did in fact exist, and that the world of the Gospels did in fact exist. No one in antiquity suggested he was mythical.

Ian Wilson ends his paperback edition of *Jesus: the Evidence* with a personal statement of belief. He acknowledges that he is a natural doubter and that he finds faith difficult. Then he sums up his position:

> With every sceptical faculty alive and kicking I *do* believe that nearly two thousand years ago, in the land we today call Israel, the "word" . . . *was* made flesh and dwelt in a Galilean Jew called Jesus . . . for a brief moment in history there was magic in the air. The sick were healed, men and women caught a glimpse of heaven, all too good of course to last.

A famous author, H. G. Wells was not a Christian. Nor was he a natural ally of the Christian Church. But his admiration for Jesus was boundless. In his famous *Outline of History* he wrote several fine pages on the impact of Jesus. I will select four sentences:

> He was too great for his disciples . . . He was like some terrible moral huntsman digging mankind out of the snug burrows in which they had lived hitherto . . . Is it any wonder that men were dazzled and blinded and cried out against him? . . . Is it any wonder that to this day this Galilean is too much for our small hearts?

The point that I am making is simple, but important. The *solidity* and *reality* of Jesus forcibly strikes each of these writers. None of them is biased in favour of Christianity. They are honest witnesses, who acknowledge that Jesus has made a tremendous impact upon them. They find him *convincing, real and "solid"* – a man with three (or four!) dimensions, not two.

He is also unique. Modern novelists often invent "solid" figures. But when they attempt to invent unique, towering figures they come up with someone like Superman. Great fun, but firmly and obviously in the world of fantasy.

On the "invention" theory we are required to believe in the unparalleled creative powers of a group of writers from the early years of the Christian era. They were prepared to suffer and die for their invention. Their achievement was so enormous that they were able to change the world. Calendars were based on their invention. Their skill was so great that their invention is able to convince modern thinkers as discerning and diverse as our witnesses.

It seems altogether more likely that they were inspired and challenged by a Real Person.

Certainly that is how it strikes me. I, at least, am persuaded that we find in the Gospels an uncontrived story, which tells the truth. To invent Jesus would require someone of the stature of Jesus. To invent the subtle differences of emphasis within the Gospels, and to relate them so subtly to the rest of the New Testament, would require a whole collective of geniuses. And genius notoriously comes in ones and twos.

CONCLUDING QUOTATION

The doubts which have been cast on the historical reality of Jesus are, in my judgment, unworthy of serious attention – *James Frazer in his famous* Golden Bough.

Note: The quotations from Josephus and Tacitus in this chapter are taken from *Invitation to the New Testament* by W. D. Davies (D.L.T. 1967). For a full account of the evidence for Jesus from ancient non-Christian sources, I recommend *Jesus and Christian Origins Outside the New Testament* by F. F. Bruce (Hodder, Second Edition, 1984).

Note: Recently, two fine books have been published with the title *The Evidence for Jesus*. The first (SCM 1985) was by James Dunn, Professor at Durham University (see page 105 for a quotation from his book). The second (Hodder 1986) is by R. T. France, Vice-Principal of London Bible College.

TAKE A BREAK (5)

Many a true word . . .
Two ministers who often disagreed met at a Unity Service.
"Still about the Lord's business, Geoffrey?" asked Philip.
"Yes," replied Geoffrey, "I'm sure we are *both* about the
Lord's business. You in your way, and me in His."

* * *

. . . spoken in jest
A young inexperienced Anglican curate was working in a
Canadian city. The bishop summoned him. "I've got a job
for you, out in the country." The curate was nervous. He
would be on his own, and hundreds of miles from home.
What would happen if he met a situation he couldn't cope
with? "Don't worry," replied the bishop. "If you get any
problems, just phone me."

Everything went very well and the curate was warmly
welcomed by the people in the villages. Sadly, one day an
elderly man died. The family invited the curate to conduct
the funeral, but on enquiring further, he discovered that
the man was a life-long Methodist. "I'd love to conduct the
service," said the nervous curate, "but first I must check
with the bishop."

"Bishop," asked the curate on the phone, "a Methodist
has died, may I bury him?"

"Go ahead, son," responded the bishop enthusiastically.
"Bury as many Methodists as you can."
(Note: my warm thanks to two Methodist friends who read
the manuscript, and allowed this story to stay in!)

* * *

A clergyman friend of mine says that he can always travel in
comfort – even in the rush hour. The trick is simple. He
travels by train, wears his dog-collar, leans out of the
carriage window at every stop, and beckons to people to

join him. It would probably work even without the dog-collar. Try it some time!

*   *   *

A Welshman dreamed that he went to heaven. "In my dream," he said, "I saw heaven as a vast choir. In the front row, stretching from east to west, there was a vast number of sopranos. Behind them, an equal number of altos. Behind them, a similarly huge crowd of tenors. And behind them, in the back row, there was *me*, singing bass all alone.

St. Peter raised his baton, and we sang "Guide me O thou great Redeemer". It was beautiful. But St. Peter wasn't satisfied; the balance wasn't quite right. So he tapped his baton and we stopped singing. Then St. Peter looked up, pointed at me and said, "A little less bass, please."

15

JESUS, BUDDHA, MUHAMMAD – WHAT'S THE DIFFERENCE?

What was Jesus *really* like?

Christianity is based, not only on ideas, but on events. At its centre we do not find a theory, but a person – the person of Jesus Christ.

He is a person who is widely misunderstood. Many people have a false, sentimental picture. To them Jesus is a rather anaemic character, more interested in flowers, birds and children than in the harsh world of adult reality.

How different is the towering figure of the New Testament! We see there a man marked out as a dangerous rebel by the authorities; a man who drew tremendous crowds; a man who inspired others to deeds of heroism; a man who took the uncompromising road to martyrdom; a man of deep passions and decisive action.

Jesus was interested in children and in nature, of course. And with the down-trodden, he was very gentle. But he was also a man among men. The world he moved in was largely a "man's world" – a harsh world of hatred, intrigue, brutality and revenge. The Gospels portray a dynamic figure who waged war against evil with the weapons of love, openness, kindness and forgiveness. Against those greatest sins of pride, hypocrisy, indifference and humbug his attack was blistering and devastating.

People fitting the above description are rare. But not unique. Other men have shown at least some of these qualities. And a few have been dynamic enough to found great religious movements – Gautama the Buddha who founded Buddhism, and Muhammad the founder of the Muslim religion, for example.

Why should we follow Christ and Christianity, rather than the Buddha and Buddhism, or Muhammad and Islam? These too were great men. Is there any real difference between them?

Are comparisons odious?

I am aware that some readers will not like the question I have just posed. In recent times the term "Comparative Religion" has given way to the "Study of World Religions". The concern is to allow people from different faiths to speak for themselves, in their own terms, without constantly making comparisons.

This shift in emphasis is one with which I have considerable sympathy. The terraced street in which I live is international and multi-cultural. We enjoy having Muslim and Bahai neighbours, and I am convinced that Christians must listen carefully to members of other faiths.

Certainly we should not attempt to score cheap points. And we must seek to present other faiths in the best possible light. *Every* faith has its share of committed, impressive members. *Every* religion – including Christianity – has its share of horror stories. "Let him who is without sin among you be the first to throw a stone . . ." (John 8:7, RSV).

The fact remains that comparisons made in a spirit of honest enquiry are sometimes inevitable. If one religion claims that a central part of its teaching is unique, that claim can only be tested by comparing it with other faiths. It is in this spirit that I now draw attention to certain aspects of Jesus' teaching.

Was his teaching original?

The answer is an infuriating Yes *and* No! *No*, because Jesus used the Jewish Scriptures as the basis for this teaching. *Yes*, because he constantly brought fresh insights, and made new connections.

For example, his code – love God with all your heart, and your neighbour as yourself – links together two separate Old Testament texts. As for the "Kingdom of God", this notion is certainly found in the Jewish Scriptures. But Jesus put it at *the centre* of his teaching, and illustrated its meaning with a series of brilliant pictures and parables.

One of the clearest examples of the uniqueness of his teaching is seen in a single word. In prayer, his fellow Jews sometimes addressed God as Father. The word they used was rather formal – as when a Victorian son called his father "sir". Jesus used a different Aramaic word: *Abba*. It was a common word in the home. It was very *un*common in prayers, for it was a child's word. "Dad" or "Daddy" is the nearest we can get.

By using that word Jesus emphasised his own close relationship with God. By encouraging his disciples to use the same word, he emphasised that our discipleship does not have its centre in a set of rules, or even in a way of life.

At its centre is a living relationship with the living God, who is *Abba*, Father.

But a loving father is not a doting uncle. The latter can make occasional visits, and indulge his nephews and nieces. A father shares his life and his standards with his children. A father's love includes discipline as well as encouragement. Hence Jesus taught us to "fear God" – to hold him in great respect, for God *is* GOD. He emphasised that forgiveness, prayer, honesty, humility and generosity are all involved in accepting God's kingly rule in our lives.

The authority of Jesus

". . . the crowds were amazed at his teaching. Because he taught as one who had authority" (Matt. 7:28,29). No doubt this striking authority had its roots in his powerful personality. But it was emphasised by the content of his teaching. A few examples will illustrate this.

1. The Sermon on the Mount: At the beginning of these three famous chapters (Matt. 5–7) we find the beatitudes. "Blessed are the poor in spirit . . . Blessed are the meek . . . Blessed are the merciful . . . Blessed are the peace makers . . ." They outline the secret of happiness – which is what "blessed" means. Jesus ends these crisp, poetic utterances with the assurance that his followers will be truly happy when they suffer "*for my sake*". When this happens they can rejoice, for their reward in heaven will be great.

In the middle of the sermon, Jesus repeats a telling phrase six times: "You have heard that it was said . . . but *I* tell you" (with stress on the "I").

The sermon ends with a vivid picture of two men: one wise, the other foolish. What is the difference between them? The wise man "hears these words of mine and puts them into practice".

2. Judgment: In various passages, such as the Parable of the

Sheep and the Goats (Matt. 25:31–46), Jesus spoke about our final destiny. He calmly assumed that it was he, Jesus, who would judge the world at the end of time.

When we recall that those to whom he was speaking acknowledged only *God* as supreme Judge, we see just how far-reaching this claim was. It is not surprising that the Jewish leaders were determined to kill Jesus, because he was "making himself equal with God" (John 5:18).

3. Worship: When the disciples worshipped him (Matt. 14:33), and when Thomas called him "My Lord and my God!" (John 20:28), Jesus accepted their worship. The tremendous difference between his attitude and that of the Apostles can be seen from Acts 14:8–18. Paul and Barnabas were horrified when the men at Lystra tried to worship them. They knew that only God is to be worshipped, and that for men to accept worship is wicked arrogance and blasphemy.

4. The Last Supper: In the synoptic accounts of the Last Supper, Jesus institutes a new covenant, "in my blood". The Bible is a book of the Covenant. It describes an "agreement" between unequals: God and his people. Six hundred years before Jesus sat down to eat with his disciples, the Prophet Jeremiah had promised that God would make a new, more glorious, covenant. By his words and actions, Jesus indicated that the great day had arrived at last – and that he, Jesus, was the central figure.

I could list more examples, but it will be as well to catch breath at this point. What does this teaching amount to? Note two points: *firstly*, it is sometimes argued that some of the great claims which Jesus made were read back into his ministry by the early Christians. Possibly: but even if they heightened the effect, *they did not invent them* – for one clear reason. They were God-fearing Jews: strict monotheists. Every day they recited the Shema: "Hear, O

Israel: THE LORD our God is one LORD" (Deut. 6: 4, RSV).
Notice: *one* LORD.

We can fully sympathise with those Jews who accused
Jesus of blasphemy. All that they had been taught demanded it. The idea of exalting a man – however great – to the
position which Jesus came to occupy in the disciples' minds
was unthinkable: dreadful. *Unless* the evidence for doing so
– *evidence presented by the Person himself* – was over-
whelming.

Secondly, Jesus did not go around saying, "I am God."
Indeed, he joyfully acknowledged his dependence upon
God. He was no usurper. But he did claim a unique
relationship with God; he did claim a unique mission from
God; and he did claim that he, and only he, could do – and
was doing – things which it was proper only for God to do.

This is put very clearly by John Robinson in *Can We
Trust the New Testament?*

> He steps in the eyes of his contemporaries into the space
> reserved for God . . . It is impossible to escape the
> conclusion that he went around not just talking *about*
> God (that would not have provoked the reaction he did)
> but standing in God's place, acting and speaking for him.
> (Page 105.)

The alternatives are beginning to emerge. They are stark
alternatives. Either this teaching is true; or it is monstrously
false. Either Jesus was blaspheming, or he was (and is) the
most significant person in all history – the one person of
whom it would not be offensive to write Person.

Before developing this point it is worth pausing to consider why it is that this teaching *about* Jesus *by* Jesus is so
easily missed – even though it is so widespread in the
Gospels. People are often surprised when it is pointed out
to them, even when they know the Gospels fairly well.

No doubt one reason is that Jesus' teaching about himself
is usually found in the course of his other teaching. He

underlines his teaching – about the Kingdom of God, or about forgiveness, or anxiety, or prayer – by reminding his hearers that he has a unique authority to speak on these matters. It seems so natural that we miss its force.

Great men don't need to boast, but they don't need to adopt an attitude of pretend humility either. If Boris Becker says, "I'm playing good tennis at the moment," he is not being conceited. He is simply speaking the truth, and, in the light of this, assessing his chances of winning at Wimbledon.

In the same sort of way Jesus, with no trace of conceit, says, "All things have been committed to me by my Father," and "Come to me, all you who are weary and burdened, and I will give you rest" (Matt. 11:27 and 28).

But I suspect that the main reason why this teaching is so often overlooked is that it is the very last thing we expect to find. We know that Jesus taught humility. He associated with, and served, ordinary people. He chose working men for his close companions. He lived a simple rough life, and he was prepared to befriend social outcasts.

To find such a humble man saying the sort of things which Jesus claimed for himself is puzzling – even shocking.

It is important to realise that Jesus, alone among the founders of the great religions of the world, spoke in this way. Muhammad and the Buddha claimed to be messengers of the Truth. Muhammad was the "Prophet of God". Gautama became "the Enlightened One" (which is what the word "Buddha" means). They felt they had a deeper insight into the Truth than most other men, and it was this insight which they wished to pass on.

Jesus claimed to be the very *source and focus of Truth*. There is a chasm of difference between these two attitudes.

Followers of other religions are just as anxious to make this clear as Christians are. The English Buddhist, Maurice Walsh, pointed out that the Buddhist view of Buddha is very different from the Christian view of Christ. He stressed that the Buddha is thought of as a Teacher – *not* as a Saviour.

The same approach applies within Islam. Dr. E. G. Parrinder made the point that Muslims "do not like the title Muhammadan", because "they do not worship Muhammad but they believe that he was the last and greatest Apostle of God". How different is Christianity! Christians glory that their name identifies them closely with Christ, whom they reverence as Teacher, Saviour and God.

Was Jesus right?
And so to the really big question. It is one thing to say the things which Jesus said. But were they true?

Notice that I have said that none of the other founders of the great religions of the world have thought of themselves as Jesus did. But I have not said that *no* other men have thought in this way.

Some rulers have claimed to be divine. Herod Agrippa I, for example (see Acts 12:19–24 for details), and some of the Roman emperors. Such rulers were usually proud, arrogant men. Even so, their claims were less far-reaching than those of Jesus. They lived in societies which believed in several gods, so it was just possible for a king to get away with such claims. Jesus and his fellow countrymen believed in *One* God. In their view, claims like those made by the emperors meant only one thing: blasphemy.

Even in modern times we occasionally find people who hold similar views about themselves. In *Basic Christianity*, John Stott recalls a letter which he received. It contained this sentence: "I have just made a great discovery. Almighty God had two sons. Jesus Christ was the first; I am the second." Sadly and predictably, the letter came from a psychiatric hospital.

It is as simple as that. Only three kinds of men could make such claims. An extremely unbalanced person who has great but false ideas about his own greatness; a liar who wants to impress people; or the one Person of whom those claims are true.

There is no fourth possibility. We cannot deny that Jesus' view of himself and his mission is correct, and in the next breath speak of him as a good man and a great teacher. If we refuse to accept his own estimate of himself, the alternatives are much harder than this.

He would not be a good man if he made these claims knowing them to be false. And he would not be a great teacher if he was wrong on this fundamental aspect of his teaching – even if he sincerely believed what he was saying. Either we accept that Jesus was the Son of God, or we number him with the world's lunatics or liars. Sane and moral men – however great they might be – do not speak about themselves as Jesus spoke.

The question which confronts us from the Gospels is clear. Was Jesus insane – falsely believing himself to be divine? Was he a blasphemous impostor – merely pretending to be God's unique Son? Or was he really the Person implied by his majestic claims?

We can easily make sense of the Buddha – he was a good, great man. We can easily make sense of Muhammad – he was a dynamic leader of men. We can easily make sense of Confucius – he was a very wise teacher. We cannot make sense of Jesus at all – unless he really is the Messiah. Or mad. Or bad.

The solution

The only way to decide this question is to examine his behaviour. Does Jesus' character measure up to his claims, or was this just big talk?

Those who lived at the time of Jesus watched him closely. Several of them came to the conclusion that his incredible claims were in fact true. They were forced to this decision by the sheer quality of his life – by the combination of sanity, wisdom, humility of life, strength, and transparent goodness.

Some of these were members of a party which opposed Jesus, and they had a lot to lose – leading Jews like Nicodemus and Joseph of Arimathea, for example. And it probably wasn't too good for the military career of the Roman centurion who supervised Jesus' execution as a criminal, to declare: "Surely this man was the (or 'a') Son of God" (Mark 15:39).

Others knew him so well and for so long, that they would have seen through a lie or a bluff. After three years of very close acquaintance with Jesus, Peter could write, "He committed no sin" (1 Pet. 2:22). We find this same thought in John's first letter: "In him is no sin" (1 John 3:5).

We too can examine his character, by reading the Gospels (St. Mark's is probably the best starting point). The issues are far too important to ignore or to shelve. If Jesus really is the Messiah; if he really is divine; if we really are a "visited planet" . . .

If . . .

If these things are true they stagger the imagination. And the practical implications are enormous.

If they are true, we are bound to revise our outlook on life in the light of what he did. We are bound to reorganise our priorities in life in the light of what he said. We are bound to give to this Jesus our obedience and worship. *If* they are true.

If we catch just a glimpse of his significance, we shall – like the wise man in the parable – build our lives on *this* Rock, and none other.

ARCHBISHOP'S POSTSCRIPT

The kind of argument which I have just developed – to point to Jesus as *the* Son of God from whom our sonship (and daughtership!) derives – is sometimes criticised on two counts. *Firstly*, on the grounds that Jesus didn't go round saying "I am God." I readily agree. His immense claims are much more subtle than this. *Secondly*, because it leans too heavily on the teaching of Jesus as recorded in the Fourth Gospel.

The teaching *about* Jesus *by* Jesus is seen at its clearest there – especially in the numerous "I am" sayings (I am . . . the bread of life; the light of life; the resurrection and the life; the way, the truth and the life, etc.). But many scholars would argue that this is *John's* way of communicating the significance of Jesus. In which case, these are not the actual words of Jesus himself.

In fact, even if it is true, this criticism does not torpedo the argument. For if we ignore St. John's Gospel for this purpose, the staggering claims of Jesus remain.

This is demonstrated very clearly in a fine book by Michael Ramsey. During a distinguished career, he was Professor of Theology of Durham University, then Archbishop of York and Canterbury. In his paperback *Introducing the Christian Faith* (now sadly out of print) he outlines several of the claims which Jesus made for himself, and for his mission. He draws on the first three Gospels only, and he concludes his argument by saying:

Consider, consider, what claims these are. Are these claims of Jesus true? If they are not true, then the making of them involves either fraud on his part or a terrible self-deception. Perhaps you are trying the line that you welcome Christ's moral teaching and admire it: but reject his own claims. It seems to me a most unconvincing line. The moral teaching and the claims are woven in one, for both concern the reign of God. I see no escape from the dilemma: either Jesus is fraudulent, or his claim is true: either we judge him for being terribly amiss, or we let him judge us. That was, in fact, the dilemma that cut through the consciences of his contemporaries.

CONCLUDING QUOTATIONS

The historical difficulty of giving for the life, sayings and influence of Jesus any explanation that is not harder than the Christian explanation, is very great – *C. S. Lewis*.

No mortal man makes such a claim, or we know him to be mad. We are driven back on the words of wise old "Rabbi" Duncan: "Christ either deceived mankind by conscious fraud, or He was Himself deluded, or He was divine. There is no getting out of this trilemma."
Christians have never been in any doubt which of these propositions is true – *Professor A. M. Hunter*.

We fall too easily into the error of underestimating the originality of Jesus. Even when he used ordinary and familiar words, he poured into them a wealth of new meaning – *Bishop Stephen Neill*.

His words carried divine authority and his actions were instinct with divine power – *Professor C. H. Dodd*.

16

DEAD MEN DON'T RISE

A story is told about Talleyrand, a leading statesman during the French Revolution. He was approached by a dejected friend, seeking advice. His friend had attempted to found a new religion. It was, he said, a considerable improvement on Christianity, but his best efforts had met with little success. What should he do?

Talleyrand paused. He agreed that the difficulties were formidable – so difficult that he hardly knew what to advise. "Still," he mused, "there is one plan which you might at least try. Why don't you get yourself crucified, and then rise again on the third day?"

Professor Sir Norman Anderson is a distinguished lawyer. He is also a Christian, and he has made a special study of the evidence for the resurrection. His faith has been sorely tested. He and his wife Pat have lived to see their three adult children die.

Their son, Hugh, was a brilliant student at Cambridge when he died of cancer at the age of 21. A few days later, Professor Anderson gave the *Thought for the Day* talk on Radio 4. After explaining why he is convinced that God raised Jesus from the dead, he continued: "On this I am prepared to stake my life. In this faith my son died, after saying 'I'm drawing near my Lord.' I am convinced that he was not mistaken."

They both understood the vital implications of Jesus' resurrection. In the New Testament it is described as the "first fruits" of a great harvest. If Jesus really *did* defeat death, then Hugh's life was not at an end. Indeed, he was making a new and glorious start.

If . . .

In this chapter we shall examine some of the evidence which convinced those two highly intelligent men. But before we do so – two preliminary comments.

1. Christianity stands or falls with this

Resurrection is not simply one aspect of Christianity. We cannot remove a portion of the Christian jigsaw labelled "resurrection", and leave anything which is recognisable as the Christian Faith: we destroy the entire picture. For Jesus himself, his cross, and his resurrection from the dead, are the three foundation stones on which Christianity rests.

People sometimes say: "I'm not bothered about questions like: did Jesus rise from the dead? We've got his marvellous teaching. Surely that's what *really* counts." This "let's-concentrate-on-his-teaching" approach is attractive. But it misses the point. *For without the resurrection it is unlikely that we would have his teaching – or anything else in the New Testament*.

In the early Church there was no preaching of Jesus *except as Risen Lord*. Nor could there be. For without the Apostles' conviction that they had seen Jesus alive again after his crucifixion, there would have been no preaching at all.

There would have been deep mourning for a lost friend. There would have been great admiration for a dead hero. No doubt his profound teaching would have been remembered and cherished by his small, loyal circle of followers. But within four generations, I suspect that he would have been forgotten.

Of course, movements do grow and develop after the founder's death – we have ample evidence of this. It happens if the founder's followers are in a buoyant frame of mind – for everything depends on their "get-up-and-go". After Jesus' death, his disciples had just about enough get-up-and-go to restart their fishing business!

Without his resurrection, at the name of Jesus every knee would not bow. More likely, people would say: Jesus who? For many men would bear that name – as they did before he came. In fact, those Jews who acknowledged Jesus to be the Messiah, *and* those who denied him, ceased to give this once-common name to their sons – for equal and opposite reasons.

For one group, the name was too high. For the other, it was too low. *Both* opinions point to the tremendous impact of Jesus – which is another way of saying that they point to his resurrection. It is an interesting commentary on the power of his name, which means "God Saves". Archbishop Michael Ramsey summed it up: "No resurrection; no Christianity."

2. Assessing the evidence is like detective work

No one claims to have witnessed the resurrection. There were people on the spot very soon afterwards, but nobody claimed that they saw God raise him up. Sorting out what happened is rather like investigating a murder case. But in reverse.

A body is found. No one saw the murder take place, but certain other related facts come to light. Jones was jealous of the victim; a bloodstained axe was found nearby; White's fingerprints were on the wallet . . . Detectives, and then lawyers and a jury, try to discover the most likely explanation for these facts. The case is decided if the explanation for each of the facts, or clues, points in the same direction.

It is the same with the resurrection of Jesus, except that the problem is reversed. We are dealing, not with someone said to be murdered, but with someone said to have come alive from the dead. No one saw what happened to the body. But certain other related facts came to light – facts which demand an explanation just as much as the axe and the fingerprints in the murder case.

We shall examine ten such facts, and try to find the most likely explanation for each of them.

First fact: Jesus died as a young man
Only a handful of men have founded great movements, and made a really decisive impact on history. Each of them needed time in which to make his influence felt. Each of them – except Jesus. For example:

Confucius (The great Chinese teacher)
  Died in 479 BC, aged 72
Gautama the Buddha (Founder of Buddhism)
  Died in 483 BC, aged 80
Muhammad (Founder of Islam)
  Died in AD 632, aged 62
Karl Marx (The great mind behind Communism)
  Died in 1883, aged 64

Now compare *and contrast* Jesus Christ. He died in AD 30, as a young man in his thirties. He spent only three years in the public eye, and those were spent in a fairly remote place. When he died he left no writing, and only a few dispirited, demoralised followers.

Yet the impact of Jesus on history has been as great as that of the great men listed above. We don't set aside one day in the year to remember him by, as with most other great figures. We base our whole calendar on his life. Every time we write the date we pay an unconscious tribute to his birth. The essayist R. W. Emerson could say that the name of Jesus "is not so much written, as ploughed, into the history of the world."

Hans Küng sums up like this: "None of the great founders of religions lived in so restricted an area. None lived for such a terribly short time. None died so young. And yet how great his influence has been . . . Numerically, Christianity is well ahead of all world religions."

This is a fact which demands an explanation. How could this village carpenter turned preacher make such a colossal impact, given his short life?

Men continue to influence the world after they are dead in two ways: through their *writings*, and through their *followers*. Jesus left no writings. True, his short earthly life made a powerful impact on his disciples. But this was largely cancelled by the shattering blow caused by his early death. So how did he do it? The New Testament answer is that *Jesus himself lived on* and continued to exert an influence, after his death.

When we read of a satellite circling the earth, we know that it was not the explosion of a child's firework which put it there. A big fact requires a big explanation. The same is true here. The continuing influence of Jesus, the startling transformation in the disciples, and the beginning of the Church which sprang from this, are "big" facts. They require a sufficiently "big" explanation. Resurrection is exactly the right size.

Second fact: several people claimed that they saw the Risen Lord

One Easter Sunday, a clergyman in Ipswich came down from the pulpit, took off his jacket, and stood on his head. When young Willy Smith told his mother what the sermon was about, she could be excused for scolding him for telling stories.

It *was* an unusual event. We do not easily accept something like that on the evidence of a single witness. But if several people claim that they saw the same thing – including several older members of the Church whose honesty is tried and tested – what then? We would be forced to accept their word about that headstand.

St. Paul wrote a letter to the Christians in the Greek town of Corinth, about twenty-five years after the death of Christ. In this letter he gave a list of people who claimed that they had seen the Lord, very much alive, after his death on the cross.

James was one. Peter was another. We can be quite certain of their honesty, for their teaching and writing were of the highest moral calibre. Besides, they were prepared to suffer and die for their beliefs (see Fact 3). Then there was the group of five hundred. Paul reminded his readers that most of these were still alive when he wrote. Their testimony could easily be checked.

We are right to view a report that someone has risen from the dead with deep suspicion. But if enough people claim to have seen him, and if other evidence points in the same direction, the situation changes. A continuing refusal to believe does not display a healthy suspicion about an unusual happening; it displays a refusal to face facts.

In his book *Jesus Christ: the Witness of History* Sir Norman Anderson records a striking example of this. He relates a conversation with a professor of philosophy, who agreed that the evidence for Jesus' resurrection is strong. But he refused to accept the evidence because "it simply could not have happened"!

Third fact: the disciples suffered for their preaching
The men who deserted Jesus to save their skins went into hiding. Then, a few weeks later, they began to preach that God had raised Jesus from the dead. They were the same men who had been crushed and shattered by his crucifixion. They were the same men who had met in secret. But they were very different same men!

In place of bitter disappointment there was joyful certainty; in place of fear there was boldness; instead of hiding behind locked doors, they were out preaching to the crowds; instead of thinking gloomily that their leader was dead, they proclaimed that he had conquered death.

In other words, they were transformed. The question is: what transformed them? They claimed that it was because God had raised Jesus from the dead. Were they right? Were they mistaken? Or were they guilty of the greatest fraud in history?

An invention? They had a motive for lying – to rescue the good name of their beloved teacher. We can imagine them plotting: "Let's steal the body, and say that God has raised him from the dead."

This neat solution founders on one fact. History teaches us that people will suffer for deeply held convictions. No one is prepared to suffer for something he has cooked up. We tell lies to get out of trouble, not to get into it! The whip and the sword soon uncover inventors. Besides, liars don't usually write high-calibre moral literature like the New Testament.

The willing suffering of the disciples also rules out the "swoon" theory. On this view, Jesus didn't die on the cross. Despite terrible wounds, he recovered in the tomb, and escaped. The disciples nursed him back to health, or tried to and failed.

This theory bristles with problems. Roman soldiers knew when a man was dead; and there was the guard on the tomb. But if we allow for a moment that this might have happened, the events which follow simply don't fit.

Jesus would have *cheated* death; he would not have *conquered* it. No doubt the disciples would have been delighted. But *they would have kept the whole thing very quiet*. Publicity and preaching would have been fatal, for it would have resulted in a search. The authorities would not have made a second mistake.

Besides, to preach that God had raised Jesus from the dead – which is exactly what they did preach – would have been a lie. We are back where we started. The lash, the dungeon and the sword would soon have loosened their tongues. Men will suffer and die for their convictions, but not for their inventions.

Fourth fact: hallucinations need certain conditions

One thing is certain. The first disciples passionately believed that Jesus had risen and that he had appeared to them. Were they mistaken? Perhaps they saw a ghost, or suffered from hallucinations.

Well, if it was a disembodied spirit or a vision, it spent a lot of time and energy trying to persuade them that it wasn't! The Risen Lord had extraordinary powers of appearance and disappearance. He didn't hide these, but he did convince the disciples that it was in his body – albeit remarkably transformed – that he came and went. They ate with him and touched him – and they concluded that God had raised him from the dead.

Perhaps the disciples were suffering from *hallucinations*? At first sight this seems more likely. But when we compare the factors involved in hallucinations with the appearances recorded in the Gospels, they don't fit. For one thing, hallucinations happen to individuals. Several people in a group – under the influence of drugs, for example – might hallucinate together. But they will experience *different* hallucinations, for these arise from the subconscious mind, and every individual's subconscious is as personal as his fingerprints.

In his book *The Day Death Died* Michael Green sifts out

six features attaching to hallucinations. Not one of these is present in the resurrection appearances. If these appearances were not inventions nor delusions it is hard to escape the logical conclusion. As John Robinson put it: "HE came to them . . . Jesus was not a dead memory but a living presence, making new men of them."

Fifth fact: they preached resurrection, not resuscitation or survival

Professor James Dunn underlines this point in *The Evidence for Jesus*. Throughout history – including Jewish history – extraordinary happenings have convinced some people about life after death. For example, ancient Jewish literature speaks of people seeing visions of their dead heroes – heroes like Abel and Jeremiah. But as James Dunn points out: "In no other case did the one(s) seeing the vision conclude 'This man has been raised from the dead.'"

I do not want to put *too* much weight on this. After all, Jesus had told his disciples that he would rise again – even though they did not grasp what he was saying. Also, many Jews believed in resurrection – but in the resurrection of *all people* on the "last day", not of *one man* in the middle of history.

So it remains true that nothing in the thought-forms of the day led them to expect the resurrection appearances of Jesus to occur in the way in which the New Testament describes them. Like so many other factors surrounding Jesus, the events are unique and unexpected.

Sixth fact: no one produced the body

The Church began, not primarily by the spreading of ideas, but by the proclamation of a fact. Something has *happened*, said the Apostles. Jesus has risen from the grave.

To disprove an idea you must argue. To disprove a fact, you must produce evidence. Those who wanted to discredit the Apostles – and the Jewish leaders wanted to do that very much indeed – had only to produce one piece of evidence to make the disciples look very silly.

All they had to do was to produce the body of Jesus. *If they had done that we would never have heard of him*, or of his followers. There would be no Church.

It is very significant that they could not do this. If the authorities had taken the body, or discovered it still in the tomb – because the disciples had lied, or had gone to the wrong grave – they would have produced the corpse. When Peter and the rest began preaching that God had raised Jesus, this would have silenced them instantly.

Instead, the authorities imprisoned, threatened, and beat the disciples. And they circulated the report that the disciples had stolen the body. It is absolutely certain that the Jewish and Roman leaders had no idea at all what had happened to Jesus. Yet the stubborn fact remains: his body had gone.

Seventh fact: the tomb was not venerated

The empty tomb is strongly supported by the fact that the grave of Jesus did not become a place of pilgrimage. Tomb veneration was common at the time of Jesus, and people would often meet for worship at the grave of a dead prophet – as they do today.

In surprising contrast, the earliest Jewish Christians did no such thing. "*No* practice of tomb veneration, or even of meeting for worship at Jesus' tomb is attested for the first Christians," affirms Professor Dunn. The practice did start up two or three hundred years later – and it persists today.

That the tomb of Jesus did not become a place of pilgrimage for the first Christians has only one satisfactory explanation. "The tomb was not venerated, it did not become a place of pilgrimage, because the tomb was empty!" (James Dunn).

Eighth fact: modern psychology supports it

By this I don't mean that most psychologists agree about

the resurrection. I mean that the considerable amount of modern knowledge about the way people behave under stress points to it.

I was ordained alongside a man who was for many years a high-ranking officer in the RAF. He explained to me how he became a convinced Christian in the first place. He was recovering from flu, and having nothing much to read, he picked up a copy of a new translation of the New Testament which his wife had bought. He began to read, and it gripped him. When he eventually put that Bible down, he was certain of one thing: the resurrection of Jesus is a fact. He saw that this was the only possible explanation for the incredible change which took place in the disciples.

He was an experienced leader of men. During the war he was awarded the Distinguished Flying Cross, and he had been a prisoner under the Japanese. He understood well how men behave under stress. He knew that dispirited people aren't creative people. He knew that men do not reassemble and organise themselves effectively, after the sort of crushing disappointment which Jesus' disciples had experienced.

A handful of frightened men would not suddenly preach boldly to the very people who had killed their leader – and so risk their own lives. Men just do not behave like that – *unless something tremendous happens to drive away the fear and disappointment.*

That wing commander was convinced that in the case of the disciples, the necessary "something" must have happened. Jesus really must have appeared to them after rising from the dead. That discovery set in motion the process which was to revolutionise his life.

Ninth fact: Christ's power today
One surprising feature of the reported resurrection appearances is that they were confined to a period of six weeks. After that they stopped abruptly. Yet the first disciples

continued to speak and behave as though Jesus was with them – not physically, but by his Spirit.

Even more remarkable is the fact that this conviction was shared by others – at first by hundreds, then thousands, then millions – who had never seen Jesus, before or after his crucifixion.

The evidence is not confined to the past. Thousands of men and women continue to experience a new power, and a continuing "presence" in their lives. Although of differing backgrounds, cultures, ages and temperaments, they put it down to the same cause: the Risen Lord is alive and at work in our world today.

The actor James Fox is a recent example of this. He was one of the "beautiful people" of the swinging sixties. He featured in several films: *Those Magnificent Men in Their Flying Machines*; *Thoroughly Modern Millie*; *Performance*. His life sounds like a cliché of the period: drugs, sex, fame and wealth.

Yet he was confused, and frightened of losing control of his life. Fitfully he read the New Testament and attended church. On Christmas Day 1968, by a series of unlikely coincidences, he met an enthusiastic Christian over breakfast in a hotel. They talked without embarrassment about the love of God, and the way of salvation. James Fox became a Christian – then he became a salesman, an estate agent, and a full-time Christian worker. He married a Christian wife and they have four children and a stable home.

After a ten-year break he has picked up the threads of his acting career. He records all this in his book, *Comeback* – described by Dirk Bogarde as "moving, and searingly honest". To summarise in a way which I think James Fox would approve: he met the living, Risen Lord, who turned his life the right way up.

Tenth fact: the evidence convinces some surprising people
Two Jewish scholars have recently studied the evidence for

the resurrection and – given their background – they have come to a remarkable conclusion. In *Jesus the Jew* Geza Vermes writes:

> When every argument has been considered and weighed, the only conclusion acceptable to the historian must be . . . that the women who set out to pay their last respects to Jesus found to their consternation, not a body, but an empty tomb.

In 1985 an orthodox Jewish scholar – Professor Pinchas Lapide – wrote a book entitled *The Resurrection of Jesus*. He surveys the evidence and concludes: "I accept the resurrection of Jesus not as an invention of the community of disciples, but as a historical event."

More than once in this book I have conceded that Christianity isn't a "tidy" religion. It is coherent and (in my view) it has the "ring of truth". But it presents us with problems and loose ends. So I am suspicious when the package presented for our inspection is *too* neat. However, I am convinced that there are few significant loose ends as far as the resurrection of Jesus is concerned – apart from our own inability or unwillingness to believe such a stupendous event.

Leslie Weatherhead likened our examination of the evidence to a journey. When all the signposts point to a particular village, then we are foolish to deny that the village exists, just because we haven't been there. If this particular village does exist – if God really *did* raise Jesus from the dead – then our own life and death begin to take on a totally new significance.

We have been sifting evidence so I will invite a lawyer – Sir Edward Clarke – to have the last word:

> As a lawyer I have made a prolonged study of the

evidence for the events of the first Easter Day. To me the evidence is conclusive, and over and over again in the High Court I have secured the verdict on evidence not nearly so compelling . . . as a lawyer I accept it unreservedly as the testimony of truthful men to facts they were able to substantiate.

17

FIVE INTO ONE WON'T GO

Before moving on we need to face one further problem for belief in the resurrection – the differences in the five acounts of the resurrection appearances in the New Testament (four in the Gospels, plus 1 Corinthians 15).

Everyone agrees that these accounts pose problems, for it is not easy to put the five together and come up with a single tidy narrative. The most recent attempt to do so has been made by John Wenham in *Easter Enigma*. (He is better known to those embarking on a study of theology by a less popular book: *Elements of New Testament Greek*!) John Wenham's book is based on a deep knowledge of modern scholarship – and of modern Israel, where he once lived.

At the other end of the spectrum are scholars who write off the task as useless. In their view it is impossible to harmonise the five accounts. Without going into details, I will make three points.

1. The evidence for the resurrection does not depend upon reducing the five accounts to one harmonious whole. Indeed, the evidence for the resurrection doesn't depend upon the finer details of the New Testament at all. It depends on something much bigger than this – finding a satisfactory explanation for the remarkable growth of the Christian Church in such poor soil.

Given the dejection of the disciples when Jesus died, together with the fact that he left no writing, the rise of the Christian movement was impossible – without a transforming factor. Those same disciples were responsible for an unparalleled burst of creative, joyful energy. This is a fact which cries out for adequate explanation.

Professor C. F. D. Moule of Cambridge sums up the problem: "If the coming into existence of the Nazarenes (i.e. the Christian Church) . . . rips a great hole in history, a hole of the size and shape of resurrection, what does the secular historian propose to stop it up with?"

2. Honest witnesses usually give different accounts of the same event – whether they are describing an accident, or a visit to the seaside, or anything else. Of course, if the accounts have a different *centre*, we are suspicious. Equally, if the descriptions are very similar, we suspect collusion.

The New Testament accounts of the events surrounding the resurrection ring true. One feature is certainly not invented. *The Gospels agree that the first witnesses were women.* In today's Iran, the testimony of a woman carries half the weight of a man's testimony. A similar viewpoint was adopted in the Palestine of Jesus. The Evangelists wanted to convince their contemporaries, but they weren't prepared to cook the books by excluding the women. "Weak" evidence like this has all the hallmarks of honesty.

3. There is a need for humility when reconstructing events at a long distance. I sometimes wonder what future historians would make of the patchy diaries of a student in England in our own century. The diary tells us that he enjoyed good health, and that he started school at Christ's Hospital, before transferring to Clifton College in Bristol. After that he went to university at the London School of Economics.

Bold minds in 2,000 years time would reconstruct his life. Clearly his statement about good health was wishful thinking, for he spent a year in hospital. And the dates which he gave for Bristol and London are muddled, for twentieth-century boys attended school *before* going to college, not the other way round. Wiser heads would counsel caution, knowing that partial information can mislead.

I will end with one very wise head from our own century. Commenting on the apparently muddled state of the accounts of the resurrection appearances, the playwright Dorothy Sayers wrote:

> The divergences appear very great on first sight . . . But the fact remains that *all* of them, without exception, can be made to fall into place in a single orderly and coherent narrative without the smallest contradiction or difficulty, and without any suppression, invention, or manipulation, beyond a trifling effort to *imagine* the natural behaviour of a bunch of startled people running about in the dawnlight between Jerusalem and the Garden.

*   *   *

Note: I have written two chapters on the resurrection without mentioning the Shroud of Turin. This is because it is not central to the evidence for Jesus' resurrection – although it *is* very fascinating.

TAKE A BREAK (6)

A vicar was surprised to receive a phone call asking him to visit the home of Mrs. Jones, who was ill in bed. He was surprised because the Joneses were a staunch Chapel family. But he was glad of an opportunity to improve the Church/Chapel relationships, and as it was August, he assumed that the Baptist minister was on holiday.

At the end of his visit he told the family how sorry he was that their own minister was away during their time of need. "Oh he's not away," replied Mr. Jones. "We called you because we thought the illness might be contagious."

*   *   *

The above reminds me of a wedding story which is believable (because people do sometimes behave very strangely in church) but unverifiable.

During a wedding service, the happy couple were kneeling at the chancel steps when the rector whispered, "And now follow me to the Communion rail." He walked the fifteen paces fairly slowly, then looked round. To his surprise they were following him as he requested – by shuffling on their knees.

*   *   *

From a Parish Magazine (so it must be true!): The best man ran into problems when he came to sign the Marriage Register in the vestry at Cawthorne, Yorkshire. The pen wouldn't write, so the vicar offered some advice (as vicars often do!). "Put your weight on it," he said. When he read the entry he was surprised to see: John Smith (10 stone 4 lb.).

*   *   *

From the Letters columns (of various magazines and papers): Until my son was four, we spent every Sunday visiting my aged father. When he died, we were able to start going to church. When a neighbour asked if we'd take her little boy to Sunday School with us, my son replied, "Oh no, he can't go to church till he's got relatives in heaven!" Further questioning revealed that he thought we were going to church so that we could talk to his grandpa. He'd been praying, "Grandfather, which art in heaven . . ." (M.P.D., Swansea).

*   *   *

"When you die, God takes care of you like your mother did when you were alive – only God doesn't yell at you all the time" (Steve K, age 8).

*   *   *

"When you die you don't have to do homework in heaven unless your teacher is there too" (Marsh, W, age 9).

Part VI

Prove it! Does God exist?

> We die on the day
> when our lives cease to be
> illumined
> by the steady radiance
> renewed daily,
> of a wonder,
> the source of which
> is beyond reason.
> *Dag Hammarskjold*

God often visits us, but most of the time we are not at home.

French Proverb

I cannot prove the existence of God, but neither can I watch a symphony orchestra at work, and believe that there is no benevolent purpose to the Creation.

Gordon McGregor

18

THIS AMAZING UNIVERSE

Does God exist? This apparently abstract question can be very practical. A young married woman wrote to a newspaper with a problem. Should she and her husband remain faithful to each other, to provide a strong family unit for their children?

It was a serious question. Would the couple find greater fulfilment by taking several "lovers"? If that woman believed that God has given us laws for our guidance and obedience – including the commandment "You shall not commit adultery" (Exod. 20:14) – she would find an answer to her very practical question.

A man who became an alcoholic and a tramp spoke movingly about his downward slide. It began as a result of guilt feelings when he became father to his girlfriend's baby. If he believed in a forgiving and merciful God, that man's life would have been very different.

No opting out: We cannot opt out of belief. Faith does not involve believing one hundred impossible things before breakfast. Christians are called "believers", but *all* people base their lives on assumptions which cannot be proved with mathematical certainty. The Christian *believes* that God exists. The atheist *believes* that God does not exist. The agnostic *believes* that there is not sufficient evidence to decide one way or the other. The indifferent person *believes* that it does not matter either way.

Recently, a high-ranking Russian defector gave a radio interview. "When I was young, when I joined the foreign ministry, I was a believer," he declared. It was when he ceased to believe in Marxism that he came to the West.

It is not a question of *whether* we believe but *what* we believe – and whether our beliefs are backed up by the available evidence. For not all acts of faith are equally well placed. Bookmakers base their livelihood on the fact that some acts of faith have more evidence to support them than others. Which is why some horses run at 100–1, and others are odds-on favourites.

What about belief in God? Is there any evidence to support this act of faith? Many reasons for faith in God have been given during human history – and in the course of this book. It is time to draw the threads together. From this mass of ideas, I will concentrate on three important areas. In this chapter we shall consider the natural world – our incredible universe.

We find evidence of order and design in the universe. Where there is design, there must be a Designer. That Designer, we call God. This sums up the famous Argument from Design (called the Teleological Argument by philosophers). We will examine the two parts of the argument separately.

1. Is there evidence of design?

A woman looked through a microscope. What she saw was so beautiful that she thought it was a diamond. In fact she was looking at the eye of a water flea – a striking combination of utility and beauty. But it can be argued that organisms like eyes have resulted from thousands of years of adaptation to the environment. So another form of this argument has been developed, which concentrates on things which cannot adapt.

A large number of factors in our world are just right to support life. If the earth was much smaller there would be insufficient gravity to hold air around our planet. If the moon was much nearer or much bigger, we should suffer from massive tidal waves, caused by its gravitational pull. If we were nearer to the sun we would fry. If we were further away we would freeze. (In fact, of course, there would be no "we"!)

The *stability* of our atmosphere is another key factor. Recently I heard a scientist puzzling over this. He was surprised that the balance of gases has remained so remarkably stable over such a long period. If the balance *did* vary, we would face enormous problems. A little less oxygen than 20.9 per cent would make breathing difficult; rather more and numerous forest fires would break out. The right balance continues – probably due to the vast network of living, breathing organisms. But experts warn that without vigilance and care, our modern way of life might do great damage in this crucial area.

Another factor which is "just right" is water. This substance – so common that we take it for granted – has some remarkable properties. It dissolves a very large number of substances (I am told that in the blood it holds over 60 substances in solution). It is not easily decomposed. It boils and freezes at temperatures which are ideally suited to the wide temperature range of our planet.

Water has extraordinary properties when nearing its freezing point. As it cools below 4°C, water *expands* – unlike other fluids, which contract. This is vital for water creatures in cold temperatures. For without this property ice would not form on the *top* of pools and rivers, but from the bottom. The expansion of water on freezing is also important for soil production – and hence vegetation – because it breaks up rocks. It is less good for lead water pipes, for the same reason!

Clearly then, a very large number of remarkable factors has come together to support life on earth. In many ways our world is strikingly beautiful and orderly. Which is not to say that *everything* is harmonious and well ordered. We have already noted the fact of *dis*harmony and the problems this raises, in Chapter 13.

2. Must there be a Designer?

Does all this mean that there must be a Designer? Unfortunately not.

It means that there *may* be a Designer. Perhaps it means that there *probably is* a Designer. But we cannot use the phrase "there must be". There is another option open to us. We may look at the universe, and maintain that it is the work of blind, mindless *chance* – things just happened to work out right. Those who believe this often say that it is the *disharmony* (suffering, earthquakes, etc.) which leads them to this view.

Some people look at the universe and say "I believe in God." Despite the areas of disharmony, they maintain that only God can account for breathtaking beauty, and for the incredible number of things which work together to make life possible.

Other people look at the universe and say "I believe in chance." It is open to them to make this act of faith. Pattern, order and surprises (like the properties of water) cannot prove beyond all doubt that God exists. The argument for God's existence, based on design in the universe, is not watertight.

If we are to get beyond the point of stalemate we must look elsewhere. In particular we must consider personal experience, and history.

CONCLUDING QUOTATIONS

In my judgment the convergence of all these factors makes it far, far more probable that God does exist than that he does not – *Bishop Hugh Montefiore.*

The ancient covenant is in pieces; man at last knows that he is alone in the unfeeling vastness of the universe, out of which he emerged by chance. Neither his destiny nor his duty have been written down – *Jacques Monod.*

The universe is full of the clatter of monkeys playing with typewriters, but once they have hit on the first line of *Hamlet* it seems that they are marvellously constrained to continue to the end of at least some sort of play – *John Polkinghorne.*

19

EVIDENCE FROM PERSONAL EXPERIENCE

A wide range of personal experiences convince people of the existence of God. I will outline and illustrate some of these.

1. General experience of the world

Geoffrey Smith is a familiar voice on radio and television – to gardening enthusiasts at least. Like many farmers and gardeners he has a strong "intuition" or "instinct" which convinces him of the existence of a Creator. The view that this world – with its abundance of life and growth – came about by chance is, to him, quite incredible.

He reminds me of another gardener: a man whose knowledge of the soil leaves him with a deep sense of wonder and gratitude – and with a sense of humour. He wryly tells the story of the gardener and the squire. "It's marvellous what you and the good Lord have accomplished between you," said the squire. "Aye," said the gardener, "but you should have seen what it was like when the good Lord had it to himself"!

2. Particular experiences of God

Frances Young is a university teacher and a mother. She teaches theology, and returns home to a severely handicapped son. In her professional life she grapples with the theological problems presented by a world in which things go badly wrong. In her private life she lives with the practical problems arising from this same fact (although I suspect that she would not describe her son as "a problem").

Frances is a radical, probing theologian. She has a colleague who recently lost his faith in God. She knows that there are no knock-down arguments for the existence of God. Yet she speaks with deep conviction of her own faith – and about certain experiences which convince her of the reality of a personal God.

One day she was sitting in a chair when she had a "loud thought". It was as though a voice said to her: "It doesn't make any difference to Me whether you believe in Me or not!" Later, when driving her car she had another "loud thought" telling her to be ordained. She can't remember the journey itself ("I must have been on automatic pilot or something"!), but she remembers the experience very clearly.

"I had the whole of my life laid out in front of me; and all its peculiar twists and turns which hadn't seemed to make very much sense suddenly fell into a pattern, as though this was all leading up to that moment and that conclusion. It was quite dramatic in its way." Frances was ordained as a minister in the Methodist Church on 3rd July, 1984.

Gerald Priestland, who records these experiences in *The Case Against God*, confesses to similar experiences of his own. He admits that "none of this can be demonstrated or transferred to anyone else, nor can anyone else persuade the experiencer that it is a delusion. In an odd way it is more real than a letter or a telephone call that could be shared." He sums up his position in two short sentences: "I hope I believe. I know that I trust."

He also describes the fascinating research into religious experience at the Research Unit based in Oxford. It is clear that more people have experiences of this kind than we might imagine – although they are often rather shy about them. 36 per cent of those questioned in a recent door-to-door survey admitted to having experiences of this sort.

3. Direct experiences of Jesus

Some people are convinced that they have "met" Jesus. Fred Lemon was a criminal: vicious, greedy and devious. One day, after a spell in the punishment block, and while he was planning a murder in his prison cell, he had three visitors. He is convinced that one of them was Jesus.

He describes this remarkable incident in his book *Breakout*, and he adds:

> When he'd gone there was this tremendous feeling that I was worth something after all; that with his help I could be the sort of person he wanted me to be. There was a great peace in my heart; it gave me the sleep of a little child . . .

The result of this encounter was a revolution in Fred's life. He left prison, and set up an open, caring home with his wife Doris – who had remained loyal to Fred through all those difficult years. They adopted five needy children. Fred became a greengrocer, thus fulfilling St. Paul's instruction to converted thieves:

He who has been stealing must steal no longer, but must work, doing something useful with his own hands, that he may have something to share with those in need (Eph. 4:28).

Archbishop Anthony Bloom has enjoyed a varied and distinguished career: as a surgeon, a member of the wartime resistance movement, and as a leader of the Russian Orthodox Church in Britain. In upbringing, culture and learning he is utterly different from Fred Lemon. But as a young man he had an experience very like Fred's.

Having heard a lecture on Christianity he was angry, and he began to read St. Mark's Gospel in order to prove that it was false. (He chose St. Mark because it was the shortest, and he didn't want to waste time on the exercise!) He relates what happened next in his book *School For Prayer*:

Before I reached the third chapter, I suddenly became aware that on the other side of my desk there was a presence. And the certainty was so strong that it was Christ standing there that it has never left me. This was the real turning point. Because Christ was alive and I had been in his presence I could say with certainty that what the Gospel said about the crucifixion of the prophet of Galilee was true, and the centurion was right when he said, "Truly he is the Son of God."

That experience had a profound effect upon the subsequent shape of his life. A deep conviction of the reality of the risen Christ has stayed with him ever since.

What are we to make of such reports? Certainly, I have never had such an experience, and because I have a large chunk of scepticism in my make-up, I look for alternative explanations. But I know Fred Lemon – he seems to me to have a well-balanced, tough personality. And having heard and read Anthony Bloom, I am struck by his deep sanity and inner stillness. They may be mistaken, but I doubt that they are given to hallucinations. And I am certain that they are honest witnesses. It is not easy to explain their experiences away.

4. Remarkable coincidences

Michael Bourdeaux is an English clergyman who speaks fluent Russian. He is Director of Keston College, a research unit devoted to helping believers in Communist lands. The way in which he was "directed" into this work is striking. In 1963 he received a letter, via Paris, in semi-literate Russian. The letter was not addressed to him, but it described the fierce persecutions under Khruschev (for example, some active Christians were confined in mental asylums).

The following year he went to Moscow, and visited the Church of St. Peter and Paul, only to find that it had been destroyed by order of the authorities. As he looked at the rubble, two elderly women were doing the same. At this point I will let Michael Bourdeaux himself take up the story.

> I addressed them in Russian. They could not have reacted more sharply if I had touched them with an electrified wire. "Oh! If you're afraid to talk, I'll leave you at once."
>
> "Who are you?"
>
> "I'm a foreigner come here to find out about the church."
>
> In a second, the hand had commissioned me. They bade me follow them – trolley, tram, a walk in the distant suburbs, an upstairs room.
>
> "Why really did you come?"
>
> "I had heard the persecution was so much worse."
>
> "Who told you that?"
>
> "I received a letter . . . from Paris."
>
> "Who wrote it?"

Hesitating, I named the two signatories.

Silence . . . a sudden flood of uncontrolled sobbing. "We wrote that letter . . . we've come to Moscow today for the second time to make contact with someone again. God sent you to meet us."

To summarise: the women had travelled seven hundred miles from their home, and Michael Bourdeaux had flown from England. Several months earlier those women had sent a letter to France which had been passed to this Englishman, whom neither of them had heard of. The writers of the letter and its recipient would not have met had either of them arrived at the demolished church an hour earlier or later.

We begin to see what Archbishop William Temple meant when he commented that when he stopped praying, coincidences stopped happening! Following their plea for help, Michael Bourdeaux launched his life's work – careful research into the facts concerning life for believers (Jewish, Muslim and Christian) in Communist lands.

5. Healings
In *The Oak and the Calf*, Alexander Solzhenitsyn describes his despair at being told that – because of cancer – he had three weeks to live. He had much to tell the world and he feared that the Soviet authorities would discover and destroy his writings. Desperately he hid his work. That was in 1953 and he continues to write today! He comments, "With a hopelessly neglected and acutely malignant tumour, this was a divine miracle; I could see no other explanation. Since then, all the life that has been given back to me has not been mine in the full sense: it is built around a purpose."

In the *British Medical Journal*, (Dec. 1983) Dr. Rex Gardner describes four recent healings, which parallel miracles recorded by the Venerable Bede twelve centuries ago. It is a detailed and impressive article. Dr. Gardner

tells of the full recovery of a young doctor who became so ill
that she was expected to die, but for whom several prayer
groups were formed, Dr. Gardner wrote: "Physicians were
unable to explain how her chest X-ray film, which had
showed extensive left-sided pneumonia with collapse of the
middle lobe, could, 48 hours later, show a normal clear
chest."

Perhaps all this will be too dramatic for some readers. If
so, I can sympathise, for I certainly don't live in a world
where this kind of thing is common. But even I sometimes
get surprises.

Two weeks ago I received a letter from a woman with
whom I had prayed at Scargill House (a Christian centre in
the Yorkshire Dales), following her course of radiotherapy. Her suspected cancer has been cured, and she believes
that God has healed her through medical science and
prayer. Doubters will no doubt see this as a shrewd means
of hedging one's bets!

I think too of Anne, a Christian probation officer who
suffered from the scourge of multiple sclerosis. She now
seems very fit, and firmly believes that God has gradually
healed her through prayer and the laying on of hands.
Others will rightly point out that multiple sclerosis is sometimes "like that". It comes and goes; it can lie dormant for
years. Anne discerns the hand of God, but proof is out of
the question. Doctors sometimes use the term "spon-
taneous remission" for unexpected recovery (in cancer, for
example). Perhaps this is a secular term for a miracle. In the
nature of things we can never be certain.

And, of course, we all know that people sometimes pray,
and remain ill or die. It would be cruel, foolish and false to
suggest that lack of healing indicates a lack of faith, or the
judgment of God.

It is my conviction that miracles do sometimes happen to
some people. If so, this is clear evidence of the existence –
and of the activity – of God. But on occasions, in his perfect
wisdom, it seems that God answers our prayers with other

words than "Yes". Words like "Wait" or "No" (Mark 14:
36 and 2 Cor. 12:8,9).

6. Experiences of God through suffering

A widow was only just recovering from the death of her
husband when she had another terrible blow: her first
grand-daughter was still-born. Her two Christian daughters
encouraged their mother to pray. One night she followed
their advice, and the next morning she woke up with a sense
of inner healing and peace. It was as though her life had
begun again. She began to experience "the peace of God
which passes all understanding" (Phil. 4:7, RSV).

Sometimes God's presence seems to bring strength
rather than peace. That was certainly the experience of
Bishop Wilson of Singapore as he was tortured (see page
126). He received strength in two ways: strength to *endure*
and strength to *forgive*.

Such experiences are not uncommon among Christians,
but they are by no means universal. C. S. Lewis wrote a
diary to enable him to cope with his grief when his wife
died. He admits that he sometimes felt desolate and alone.

He did not write glowingly about experiencing God's
presence. But he recalled Jesus' cry of dereliction on the
cross: "My God, my God, why have you forsaken me?".
He came to see more deeply into St. Paul's affirmation (2
Cor. 5:7) that we are called to walk by faith, not by sight –
nor, ultimately, by feelings and emotions, either.

Sometimes the courage of those who suffer is
tremendously moving. Recently I received a letter from a
friend who was forced to take early retirement as a result of
multiple sclerosis. She wrote:

> I've had to give up driving. The fatigue is rotten, but
> not such a worry now that I've stopped working.
> The blurred and double/triple vision is a nuisance, but
> curiously interesting, e.g. the Cathedral has had 2 spires

for a couple of years; there are 3 moons in the sky and an awful lot of 8-legged cats about!

I am quite used to it now and it's not a worry.

I've made no retirement plans, confident that something will emerge for me, when the time is right.

7. Encounters with holiness

Michael Dummett is Professor of Philosophy at Oxford University. He took over from England's best-known atheist – Professor Sir "Freddie" Ayer – who admires his successor's mind and ability, but strongly disagrees with his Christian Faith!

One reason which convinces Professor Dummett is that he finds truly holy people within the Church. Alas, not every Christian, by any means. But some people have a depth, a serenity and a joyful goodness which points him to God. John Polkinghorne makes a similar point in his book *The Way The World Is*:

> I have to say that in my experience most of the people I know who impress me most as being open to reality, deep in perception, firm in love, are also Christian believers. Of course, not all. I gladly acknowledge these qualities in friends who stand outside the faith. But there does seem to be a special quality in people who live close to God.

He goes on to give specific examples.

8. Friendship

Related to this is the remarkable experience of Christian friendship. I am extremely fortunate in having many fine friends. Some are believers; some are not. I am bound to say that I am struck by the fact that friendships with fellow Christians often (not always) achieve greater depths. There is a spirit of joyful, mutual understanding, which arises from sharing a common faith.

The New Testament often talks in corporate terms.

Christian disciples do not pursue a lonely pilgrimage. *Together* they form the body of Christ, and the family of God. This actually works out in experience. Phrases like "in Christ", "brotherly love" and "fellowship in the Holy Spirit" are not clichés. Even though we often fail, and relationships sometimes break down, the depth of many Christian friendships points to the reality of their conviction that their unseen, Risen Lord is the most important person within the group.

Bishop Stephen Neill was a Christian leader and teacher in many continents, over many decades. Shortly before his death in 1984, he testified movingly to the enduring quality of friendships made across the world. He concluded: ". . . perhaps Christians are right in thinking that Jesus revealed new dimensions of friendship, and that he is himself the element of permanence in friendship between those who believe in him" (from *The Supremacy of Jesus*: Chapter 7 is devoted to this subject).

I recognise that these are a dangerous couple of paragraphs. They may seem suffocatingly "cosy" to those outside the Faith. If so, I am sorry. But I have decided to take the risk, for over the years the force of this experience has struck me time and again. And I am aware that this section will ring bells for many Christians who have never had a "remarkable" experience.

9. Undramatic experiences

At this point, space requires that I draw this chapter to a close. Selection has been inescapable, but I hope that I have given enough examples to enable you to weigh up this aspect of the evidence for the existence and activity of God.

Perhaps it will ring bells in your experience. Perhaps it will not. I have described some remarkable examples, and this might be a mistake. For many people have a strong faith in God without undergoing dramatic experiences. For some, the main pointer is a quiet confidence that they are "accompanied", "helped" and "directed" through life by an unseen Presence – and challenged, too, to acts of love and service.

No doubt the material in this chapter will drive some readers to put this book down, and to reach for a manual in psychology or sociology! Even there you might not be quite safe. Peter Berger, a leading American sociologist, has written a brilliant book (*A Rumour of Angels*) in which he suggests that ordinary experiences like fear, comfort, hope and humour, point to God.

A good deal of what I have said can be summed up in one short sentence from the Gospels. "For where two or three come together in my name, there am I with them" (Matt. 18:20). Millions of ordinary believers, who have never had a "special" experience of God, will testify that these words of Jesus sum up their experience. They stubbornly affirm that they meet for prayer, worship and fellowship, not to remember a dead hero, but to meet – *and to be met by* – a living Person. Their testimony is impressive.

CONCLUDING QUOTATIONS

I am unable to see how a man can find the hand of God in secular history, unless he has first found that he has an assurance of it in his personal experiences – *Professor Herbert Butterfield*.

Science must admit the psychological validity of religious experience – *Sir William Cecil Dampier*.

In his autobiography, Lord Clark (who died in 1980) described a religious experience. It is both moving and sad, and it shows that such experiences require a response. It also shows that refusal to respond is, in itself, a form of response.

I had a religious experience. It took place in the Church of San Lorenzo, but did not seem to be connected with the harmonious beauty of the architecture. I can only say that for a few minutes my whole being was irradiated by a kind of heavenly joy, far more intense than anything I had known before. This state of mind lasted for several months, and, wonderful though it was, it posed an awkward problem in terms of action. My life was far from blameless: I would have to reform. My family would think I was going mad, and perhaps after all, it *was* a delusion, for I was in every way unworthy of receiving such a flood of grace. Gradually the effect wore off, and I made no effort to retain it. I think I was right; I was too deeply embedded in the world to change course. But that I had "felt the finger of God" I am quite sure, and, although the memory of this experience has faded, it still helps me to understand the joys of the saints – *From: The Other Half: A Self-Portrait Kenneth Clark: 1977 (Page 108)*.

20

EVIDENCE FROM HISTORY

Those who have known experiences of the kind I have just described find them compelling. To them they provide unshakeable evidence for the existence of God. But those to whom such experiences are foreign often find these accounts less convincing. So we move now to the third strand of evidence, which is, I believe, strongest of all.

By "the evidence from history" I mean especially those events which took place in the middle decades of what we now call the first century AD or CE. The evidence is not confined to those years – but it is at its strongest there. All we need to do at this point is briefly to recap four previous chapters (14–17).

1. In the course of his teaching, Jesus made far-reaching claims about himself. Despite this, his life-style was simple, and his manner was humble. He rings true. Here is no boaster, puffing himself up. On the contrary, he is more interested in serving than in being served. In particular he wants to reach out to the ordinary people of his day, and to those outcasts whom even these peasants regard as beyond the pale.

All the evidence points strongly in one direction. Jesus is indeed the unique Son of God. If he *is*, then the God of whom he is the Son, must exist. Hence the question "Does God exist?" resolves itself into a question about Jesus. Equally important, the vital questions "What is God like?" and "Does God care?" do the same. For Jesus is a living "visual aid". He points us to God. "No one has ever seen God, but the only begotten Son . . . has made him known" (John 1:18). "Like Father, like Son". The keynote of his character is strong love.

The phrase "Sons of God" is also used in the New Testament to refer to those who – through faith in Jesus as the Risen Lord – have entered the family of God. But there is a clear difference between these two uses of the term. It is *his* sonship which makes *ours* possible. We are God's children "by adoption" (Rom. 8).

If we reject Jesus' own estimate of himself, we run into severe problems. The difficulty of finding a satisfactory alternative explanation for his teaching is tremendous. It might be possible for me to imagine that I am the world's greatest footballer – brilliant, but unrecognised – and to remain sane. It would be totally impossible to falsely believe that I have a unique relationship with God the Father, and a mission of incomparable significance, and to remain sane.

Either we accept Jesus' own estimate of himself – and

hence accept that God exists – or we must write him off as a liar, or as a madman. His character, behaviour, and moral teaching, make these last two explanations extremely difficult to accept. To get round the problem, we invent a fourth category. Jesus is not divine; nor was he a liar or a madman. He was a good man and a great teacher – and nothing more. But this is a mirage. It will not stand up under investigation.

On one occasion, because of his hard teaching, large numbers of would-be followers left him. Jesus turned to the inner circle and asked if they would leave too. Peter replied, "Lord, to whom shall we go? You have the words of eternal life" (John 6:68). I for one believe that answer to be profoundly true.

2. The New Testament also claims that God raised Jesus from the dead. If this is true, we are yet again forced to the conclusion that God is active in our world. So once again, what appears to be a vast theoretical question about the existence of God, is in reality a historical problem. A problem about making sense of Jesus, and of the way in which Christianity began.

If the evidence outlined in Chapter 16 is correct, we have our answer. God does exist. We know this because he sent his Son to us, and his Son gave his life for us. When men crucified him, God raised him from the dead. This is the central Christian claim, and pages 135–174 form the core of this book.

In addition to proving God's existence, the resurrection highlights three aspects of his character: he is the source of Life, of Joy, and of wonderful Surprises.

In the light of this, the fact that we find design in the universe takes on a new significance. We may not believe in God *because* of design. But if we believe in God because of Jesus Christ, then we learn that the harmony and pattern is, after all, due to God.

Feel the firm earth under your feet. Ponder the fact that it is moving in orbit round the sun at about 100,000 kilometres per hour. Look at the heavens, and remember that light from the nearest star takes over four years to reach earth – and light travels at 186,282 miles per second.

Enjoy the scent, colour and intricacy of a delicate flower. Consider the beautiful simplicity of the recurring pattern of the seasons. Contemplate the fact that underlying it all is a complexity so great, that the world's scientists constantly need to review and revise their findings.

The God who cares for us; the God who came to us; the God with whom we can communicate in prayer; the God who will give to our lives both meaning and power, if we will allow him – he it is who designed, and who created, and who upholds, all things.

If we can be moved by anything, this will move us. With the Psalmist we will declare:

> Great is the Lord and most worthy of praise; his great-
> ness no one can fathom.
> One generation will commend your works to another;
> they will tell of your mighty acts (Psalm 145: 3–4)

TAKE A BREAK (7)
RATHER MORE SERIOUS

The story is told of a man who walked too near the edge of a cliff. He fell off, and as he plunged down, he put out his hand and hung on to a thorn bush growing from the cliff face. He looked up: the cliff was too high to climb. He looked down: it was far too far to fall!

In desperation he looked up again and shouted, "Is there anyone there?" To his delight, there was an answering voice. "Yes, I – the Lord your God – am here." "What shall I do?" called the man. After a pause, the voice replied, "Let go." The man looked down at the rocks 100 metres below. Then he looked up, and called out again, "Is there anyone *else* there?"

* * *

This final *Take a Break* has a sting in the tail. I suggest that *we* are rather like the man on the cliff. We look at the world around us – at its beauty, and at its chaos – and we wonder, "Is there anyone there?"

We receive our answer. "Yes, *I* am here: the Lord your God, revealed in Jesus Christ."

Like the man in the story, we are alarmed. For this is not the God we want. *This* God makes tough demands. He tells us that we must deny ourselves; that we must take up a cross, and follow Jesus. He insists that we cannot – must not – live for ourselves; that I *am* my brother's keeper. He calls us to a life of faith – insisting that we stop trusting in perishable things (our savings, our health, our work . . .) and trust in him alone.

Like the man on the cliff, we do not like what we hear. So we call out again: "Is there anyone *else* there?" But there isn't. It is *this* God, or no God at all.

Unlike the man on the cliff we have good reason to heed that voice. Above all, we have the promise of Jesus who said: "Do not be afraid, little flock, for your Father has been pleased to give you the kingdom" (Luke 12:32).

This is the message of the Bible. It brings deep comfort. It also carries strong demands. The main thrust of its message is all too clear. Mark Twain spoke for most of us when he said that it wasn't the parts of Scripture that he *didn't* understand that worried him. It was the parts that he *did* understand that were the trouble!

Of course there is an easy way out of Mark Twain's dilemma. I once heard of a man who was very disturbed when he kept reading about the connection between smoking and lung cancer. So he resolved there and then to give up. He stuck to his resolve, and throughout his short life, he never touched a book again.

21

THE CASE AGAINST INERTIA

It is my conviction that "The Case Against Christ" is not strong. The evidence *for* him is very strong indeed.

It is vitally important to keep the discussion about Christianity centred on this question of evidence.

"His hobby is gardening. My hobby is fishing. Your hobby is religion." Such an attitude is common but inadequate. Christianity just won't fit into a list of hobbies or interests. It is far too big for that.

People follow Jesus for a variety of reasons. Some, because they have a keen sense of sin and know that they need forgiveness and moral power. Some because they feel inadequate to deal with life, and know that they need help. Others because they are deeply impressed by the life of a particular Christian or group of Christians. Yet others because they read the New Testament and are convinced that Jesus Christ is the Son of God.

All these are valid reasons. But the *primary* reason for becoming a Christian, which underlies them all, is that *Christianity is true*.

A personal note will be appropriate here. The *basic* reason why I am a Christian is not because I have a religious temperament (I'm not sure that I have); nor because I find it convenient (its moral teaching is often extremely *in*-convenient); nor because it brings comfort (although it does); nor even because I find in it the strength which I need to live my daily life (although I do).

I am a Christian because I am convinced that the Christian Faith is *true*.

I am persuaded that the Jesus of the Gospels rings true. I am further persuaded that in him, love and hatred, light and darkness, life and death have contended – and that he is Victor, Lord and King.

If anyone could show me that Christianity is not true, then I would have nothing more to do with it.

We are not dealing with a matter of personal taste, but with a question of truth or falsehood. Either Jesus *is* the Son of God, or he is not. Either he *did* rise from the dead or he did not. Either he *is* alive and able to help us today, or he is not.

But in my experience most people do not apply the test of truth. Instead they are influenced by the spirit of the age, by the opinions of family and friends, and by the widespread indifference to Christianity. The words of G. K. Chesterton continue to be true: "The Christian ideal has not been tried and found wanting. It has been found difficult; and left untried."

Practical: The fact that the central question concerns truth and straight thinking does not mean that Christianity is mere theory – and so without practical implications.

A few years ago I discovered that a woman in a crinoline probably introduced overarm bowling into cricket (try bowling in one and you will see why!). It is perfectly appropriate to follow such a discovery with the comment, "How interesting." Other discoveries – that your house is on fire, or that you have inherited a fortune – must be followed by positive action.

The discovery that Christianity is true comes into the second category. To accept Christ because he is the Truth involves a revolution in our behaviour and moral standards, and in our entire outlook on life – for Jesus comes with tough demands.

He comes, too, with unutterable comfort. To a world beset by problems he comes as guide. In a world where many are lonely, he comes as friend. To a world which often seems to lack meaning, he brings understanding. Over a world where dying is the single certainty, he sits enthroned as the conqueror of death.

The words of Jesus, as recorded by St. John, have been tested and proved in the lives of countless thousands of men and women: "I am the light of the world. Whoever follows me will never walk in darkness, but will have the light of life" (John 8:12).

POSTSCRIPT: WHERE NOW?

One reader of the typescript suggested that I should write a final note for those readers who want to turn vague good intentions into decisive action. He had in mind those readers who are convinced that Jesus Christ is the Light and Saviour of the world – and those who are uncertain, but keen to keep the enquiry going. With such people in mind I would like to highlight four universal needs.

1. *We all need inspiration, direction and challenge.* So I want to encourage you to read the Bible – and especially the Gospels, where you can meditate on the life and teaching of Jesus. I suggest that you start with St. Mark, then read a few of the New Testament letters. A modern translation makes the text much clearer.

2. *We all need friendship* – one good reason for going to church. In addition to finding friendship you will learn more about the Christian Faith through sermons, and more about the Christian family through experiencing its love – and its faults!

3. *We all need forgiveness and strength.* So we need to pray. "Lord, have mercy on me, a sinner" is a good prayer to start with. Other people need help too. One way of loving them is to pray for them.

4. *We all need markers in our lives.* It often helps to make a definite move. So if you are clear that you want to launch out on the Christian life, or if you want to recommit yourself to Christ, I suggest that you take a piece of paper and write on it something like "On this day . . . I make a Covenant with God. Signed . . ." On the same piece of

paper you might care to write out a prayer or a Bible verse.
If you decide to do this, I suggest that you do two further
things. Lend this book to a friend, as a small act of Christian
witness. And write to me c/o Hodder and Stoughton, 47
Bedford Square, London – for I should like to pray for you.

*   *   *

Grace and peace be yours in abundance through the
knowledge of God and of Jesus our Lord (2 Pet. 1:2)

OUR GOD IS STILL TOO SMALL

John Young

What is God like? Analysing popular myths and misconceptions about God, John Young shows how our understanding of God has practical implications for the way we live our lives, the way we view the world, and for our peace of mind – or lack of it.

'This book could disturb you, give you sleepless nights, and even push you into actually doing something about your faith.'
Margaret Cundiff, from her foreword

'As soon as I started it, I couldn't put it down. I think it's a splendid book, racily written, readable and entertaining, yet profound, thought provoking and at times extremely powerful.'
Joyce Huggett

'This book deals with a subject vital to our day – I recommend it.'
Clive Calver

'John Young has great skill in perceiving the deep issues facing people who try to take Christianity seriously. As well as helping those who wrestle with the problems, he will provide inspiration to those who help other people to wrestle in this way.'

Donald English

KNOW YOUR FAITH

John Young

The excitement of Christian truth presented afresh in an eight-week study of the Apostles' Creed.

'I am delighted to commend John Young's book warmly. *Know Your Faith* will be a major resource for parish groups and individuals.'
George Carey, Archbishop of Canterbury

'Anyone who sits in on a group which follows these eight investigations into the Apostles' Creed (or, better still, spends sixteen sessions on them, for they contain so much good material) will end up as a more informed and more intelligent Christian than when they began.'
John Taylor, Bishop of St. Albans

'John Young has a great gift for communicating profound ideas simply and readably. His skills were never more needed as the churches launch into the Decade of Evangelism.'
John Habgood, Archbishop of York